Thread of Gold

Thread of Gold

The Embroideries and Textiles in York Minster

Edited by Elizabeth Ingram

Pitkin Pictorials

Acknowledgements

Photographs by Jim Kershaw, York, copyright the
Dean and Chapter of York except for: Figs 2, 3 and
56a © Peter Gibson reproduced by kind permission of
the Dean and Chapter of York; Fig. 5 © Society of
Antiquaries of London; Fig. 17 © the Museum of
Applied Art, Oslo; Figs 42, 45, 69a and 69b
© Lt. Col. Jack Allen; Fig. 52 © Mr Derek Phillips,
University of York; Figs 54a, 54b, 55a, 55b and 55c the
late Gwendoline Strafford, © Clare Strafford; Figs 58
and 70 © Ken Baldwin.

The Dean and Chapter of York acknowledge with
thanks the financial support of the Friends of York
Minster in producing this book.

First published in Great Britain 1987
by Pitkin Pictorials Ltd
North Way, Andover, Hants SP10 5BE

© The Dean and Chapter of York

Printed in Singapore
by Tien Wah Press

Designed by Adrian Hodgkins

British Library cataloguing in publication data

Thread of gold: the embroideries and textiles
    in York Minster
    1. York Minster   2. Ecclesiastical
    embroidery—England—York (North
    Yorkshire)
    I. Ingram, Elizabeth
    746.44′09428′43   NK9310

ISBN 0 85372 427 X

FRONT COVER   *Detail from the Benedicite
chasuble, c. 1920. See p. 46.*

FRONTISPIECE   *The head of Christ (detail) from
the Great Processional Banner, c.1914–16. See pp. 38–41.*

Contents

Foreword

Dean Milner White wrote in the 1955 Friends' Report,

like our ironwork and precious metalwork, they [the textiles] *deserve a descriptive booklet all to themselves.*

Here it is. It is a work of art in itself.

We owe a debt of gratitude to those who take care to see that our treasures are looked after and properly recorded. In this volume the reader will detect the hand of someone who has been deeply involved in the creation of new treasures of embroidery as well as recording those which we have inherited.

This will be a valuable book to possess as well as being a guide to what there is to be seen in York Minster and I am sure that you will find it another treasure to enjoy.

John Southgate, Dean
York 1987

Introduction

A golden thread runs through ecclesiastical embroideries and textiles from the earliest recorded times and it is still as much in evidence today.

This book sets out to cover a comprehensive selection of the Minster's embroideries and textiles which will be of general interest, but it is not a complete inventory.

Many examples of work are visible at all times when the Minster is open to the public, others are changed according to the liturgical seasons but some, especially those of historic age and interest, are kept in storage.

In the future it is hoped that facilities will become available so that more of the Minster's treasures may be displayed for the enjoyment and interest of visitors.

The information given in this book is up to date to the time of writing but research constantly throws new light on the collection. For instance, just before this book went to press, an exciting discovery was made in a Minster storeroom: three fragments of tapestry were found, each about 70 cm square, which are probably nearly 600 years old. Two of them bear the arms of Scrope of Masham (the Scropes were great benefactors of the Minster in the early 15th century) and the third piece shows the greater part of a falcon rising – a badge of the Scropes. Preliminary research points to an early 15th century date and an inventory of 1500 records '12 pieces of red bearing the arms of the Lord Scrope hanging in the choir'. The '12 pieces of red' are mentioned again in 1690 by James Torre who both described and illustrated the devices.

Many people have been of the greatest help in putting the contents of this book together and I would specially mention Dr Sylvia Hogarth who is engaged in zoological research at the University of York. Sylvia has had a life-long interest in embroidery and historical research. Robert Patterson, B.Sc., F.M.A., former curator of the Castle Museum, York, is an old friend and his interest and expertise in unravelling the complexities of the tablet-woven braids from the tomb of Archbishop Walter de Gray and then weaving the facsimiles almost defies belief. Miss Natalie Rothstein, Acting Keeper of the Textile, Furnishing and Dress department at the Victoria and Albert Museum and her staff have been most generous of their time and knowledge, without which it would have been difficult to identify and date many items.

I would also like to thank Lt. Col. Jack Allen, Mrs Ida Barber, Mr Bernard Barr, Sub Librarian, York Minster Library (University of York), Mr Richard Bunday, Head Verger and his staff, Dr and Mrs Eric Gee, Mr Peter Gibson, York Glazier's Trust, Mr Charles van der Heyden, the Very Revd Ronald Jasper, Dean Emeritus of York, Mevrouw E. F. Kalf, Jur. Dra. Haarlem, the Revd Canon Adrian Leak, Mr David Peace, F.S.A., Mr Derek Phillips, University of York, Mr Peter G. Redfern, Mr M. Smith and his staff at York Central Library, Mr Irvine Watson, Miss Yvonne Weir and Mrs Carolyn Wood.

Without the encouragement and support of the Dean and Chapter of York this book would never have been written.

C.E.I.
March 1987

Ecclesiastical Vestments at York Minster Before the Reformation

Sylvia Hogarth

York Minster has a long tradition of fine vestments as well as of other rich treasures. While the development of the present building has been one of cumulative growth since the 11th century the history of the ornaments of the church falls into two periods; pre- and post-Reformation. The vast accumulation of vestments, gold and silver ornaments, jewels, relics, books and images built up over the centuries was destroyed or dispersed between 1541 and 1553. The Minster possesses some fragments of textiles that survived the Reformation; two tablet-woven bands and the remains of a cushion recovered from the tomb of Archbishop Walter de Gray who died in 1255 (see pp. 19–22).

Thus this book falls into two sections; the introduction based largely on archival material, deals with the earlier period while the major part describes textiles acquired more recently.

Ecclesiastical costume has evolved from the everyday wear of the Roman citizen of the 1st and 2nd centuries AD. Many garments worn by the clergy are little changed from this period. While secular fashions changed, ecclesiastical styles were very conservative. Up until the 9th century there was some development in the vestments but in the transitional period between the 6th and 9th centuries the form of most of the garments was codified either by Papal declaration or by ecclesiastical councils; the Fourth Council of Braga in 675 AD issued a decree which regulated the way in which the *orarium* (stole) is worn by priests.

It is possible to understand how the vestments were worn by looking at paintings, manuscripts, monumental brasses and stained glass. Figure 1 shows Sir Simon Wensley, *c.* 1360, in his Eucharistic vestments and holding the chalice, both of which indicate that he is a priest. This detailed brass shows very clearly the early shape of the most important of the Mass vestments, the *chasuble*. This large garment was originally circular in shape with an opening for the head. It developed from the Roman 'overcoat', the *paenula*, which was also known as the *casula*

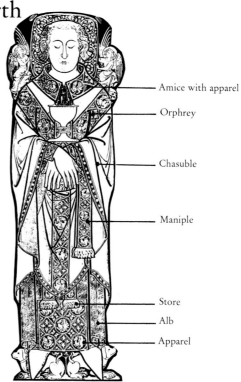

FIGURE 1   *Sir Simon Wensley c.1360 wearing Eucharistic vestments. Brass in Holy Trinity Church, Wensley, North Yorkshire.*

(little house), hence the derivation of the word *chasuble*. This vestment was usually made of rich fabric such as silk and was frequently embellished with decorative bands, the *orphreys*. The word *orphrey* is a version of *auriphrygium*, Latin for gold embroidery. This in turn was derived from Phrygianus – the Phrygians, from Asia Minor, were considered great embroiderers by the Romans. Orphreys were sometimes made of a different rich fabric which contrasted with the background fabric or were elaborately embroidered with various motifs or scenes from the life of Christ. Simon de Wensley's chasuble has a narrow hem orphrey and a much wider, Y-shaped central orphrey. The shape of the central orphrey varied; some were a simple central pillar on the front and back, some also had diagonal stripes to the shoulder and some were cross-shaped.

For the purposes of the Mass where the priest must raise his arms, the full chasuble is a cumbersome and heavy garment. In some pictures, the chasuble is shown with the fullness folded up over the shoulders. Over hundreds of years the garment became much slimmer and then the embroidery covered most of the fabric.

Under the chasuble the priest would wear an *alb*. This evolved from the loose Roman undertunic, the *tunica linea*, and was usually made of white linen although coloured albs made of silk, cloth of gold and velvet are recorded. Over the years, the shape of the alb also became slimmer and in particular the sleeves became tighter fitting. The alb was worn by all officers of the church from the doorman to the archbishop. Albs were frequently decorated with ornamental patches of embroidery known as *apparel*. Two patches were sewn on the lower portion of the alb, front and back (Fig. 1). Two patches (unseen) were sewn on the chest and back and one on each cuff. Early cuff apparel circled the whole wrist as can be seen on the alb of Simon de Wensley. A narrow ornamental strip might also edge the neckline; this neckstrip would not be seen as it was masked by the *amice*, a separate collar evolved from a hood, which was made of a plain fabric, but had an ornamental strip, also called an apparel, at its top edge. Eventually this was no longer used as a head cover, but the plain fabric was folded behind the stiffened ornamental band.

Hanging from the priest's left wrist is a slip of decorated fabric, the *maniple*, also known as the *fanon*. This developed from the *sudarium*, a towel originally used by the priest to wipe his face during the service (*sudor* – sweat). Another long narrow strip of decorated fabric with fringed ends, the *stole* or *orarium* was worn around the neck, crossed over the chest, held in place by the girdle and hung to the hem of the alb under the chasuble. As can be seen in the brass, the decorated bands of orphrey, apparels, maniple and stole are all a matching set. York Minster inventories also list sets of matching vestments: '*una casula de baudekin cum stole, fanona, spaulers et paruris de eodem secta cum amica de serico alterius coloris*' – a chasuble of cloth of gold with stole, maniple, shoulder patches and apparel of the same set with amice of other coloured silk.

The officiating priest might be assisted at the Mass service by a deacon and subdeacon. The deacon would wear an alb and a dalmatic and the subdeacon an alb and tunicle. The *dalmatic* and

FIGURE 2 *St. Peter c.1325 wearing the vestments of an archbishop including the pallium. The Pilgrimage window, North nave aisle.*

tunicle were similar to the alb in shape, but shorter and narrower with side slits which might be decorated with fringes. The dalmatic would usually be made of a rich fabric but the tunicle of a plain fabric. The chasuble, dalmatic and tunicle would constitute a suit of vestments – 'A vestment of whyte damaske and all thinges for dekyn, and subdekyn of the same'. Here the 'vestment' is used in its strictest sense to mean the chasuble.

Bishops and Archbishops would wear the alb, tunicle, dalmatic, chasuble and *mitre*. In this case the tunicle would also be of a rich fabric with fringe. The Archbishops would also wear the *pallium* or *pall*. This was a narrow strip of fabric worn around the shoulders with a strip hanging at the back and at the front. The pallium was always made of white wool decorated with black crosses. An Archbishop was expected to travel to Rome to receive his pallium directly from the Pope and so symbolically demonstrate his allegiance to Rome rather than to the Archbishop of Canterbury or the English monarch. Latterly he was also expected to pay a large sum of money for the pallium. Figure 2 shows St. Peter in the vestments of an Archbishop, including his pallium, in the stained glass of the Minster's Pilgrimage window in the North nave aisle.

As well as the vestments worn for the services of the sacraments, there were other garments worn and also rich and ornamented fabrics used to decorate the altars.

The *cope* became one of the richest of ecclesiastical garments. Originally a form of outer cloak worn by everyone, it developed into a magnificent processional garment. Because it was not a sacerdotal vestment, it was one of the few ecclesiastical garments that was not prohibited at the Reformation. Copes were frequently dec-

FIGURE 3   *Sir Richard Yorke, 15th century, kneeling on a cushion by an altar covered with a decorated cloth. North transept.*

orated with orphreys in the form of decoration down the straight front edges of the cope. In addition, the flat, shield-shaped panels at the back of the neck, which had evolved from the hoods, were richly ornamented. The decoration of orphrey and hood was usually embroidery either with repeating motifs of scenes from the life of Christ or of the saints. These were often embroidered in gold thread in the famous *Opus Anglicanum* technique which flourished from the 12th to the 14th century. These English embroideries were in great demand and many are still found in museums in England and on the continent.

The cope was held in position by a clasp, the *morse*, which was embroidered or made of gold or silver set with precious stones. Many were very large and might depict a religious scene.

Rich cloths were also used to embellish the tops and fronts of altars and as curtains at the back and sides. As well, there would be embroidered items used for *burses*, *veils* and *corporals*. Figure 3, from the Minster North Transept windows, depicts Sir Richard Yorke kneeling on a cushion by an altar that is covered with a decorated cloth and has a frontal made of a textile with a different design.

The fabrics used for garments and altar decorations were very varied and often costly and imported. It is possible to discover some of the detail of the fabrics and their use by study of the various inventories of the possessions of the Minster that were made at different times. One very full inventory was made in the early 1550s. As well as these inventories made at the time, there is also another very valuable list made from archival material. In 1859, James Raine, a York historian, published *A List of the Chantries within the Cathedral Church of York*. In this he compiled information from the Chapter Books from the 14th to the 16th century which give details of the furniture, furnishings and vestments belonging to the many chantry shrines in the Minster. The examples below, quoted from these inventories, describe something of the range and richness of the vestments.

The richest textile was cloth of gold, a fabric made of silk with gold threads woven in; baudkin and samet were variations of this gold fabric while tissue was silk woven with gold or silver threads:

> 'j vestimentum de panno aureo'
> 'unus pannus de serico albo deaurato'
> 'a vestment de blodio bawdkyn de panno aureo'
> 'casula rubia de samito'
> 'iij capae de albo ruceto velvet tyssue'.

There were a number of different kinds of silks used such as sarsenet, changeable silk, syndone, camaka and taffetta:

> 'una bursa de serico cum reliquiis'

> 'unum sudarium de syndone'
> 'ij tuniculus veteribus de sendall'
> 'unum vestimentum de syndone'
> 'sex pulvinaria de viridi sateyn figurata cum le trefoyles'.

The name of the fabric is often an indication of its country of origin; *baudkin* is a corruption of Baghdad. It does not necessarily mean the fabrics themselves came from the named country or town; for example *damask*, which originally came from Damascus, was made in a number of cities in Italy in the 15th and 16th centuries. Some fabrics had exotic names that are not at all informative about their composition, such as *burd Alexandria*.

> 'a vestment de water damaske de nigra'
> 'two copes of clothe imperialle'
> 'duo panni de blodio tartari' [silk from Tartary/China]
> 'tria corporalia de panno de reynes' [cloth from the Rhine]
> 'one westment of darnecks' [from Doornick (now Tournai)]
> 'unum vestimentum de borde Alisaundre'

Other fabrics were of English manufacture:

> 'iij alterclothis of twyll and ij of playne cloth'
> 'ij alterclothison of diaper and a noder of playn cloth'
> 'j pulvinar de panno lanio operis tapistre'
> 'on vestment of blake fustyan' [like velveteen/corduroy]
> 'j vestimentum de nigro velvet'
> 'a vestment de veridi worsitt cum rubia cruce' [from Worsted in Norfolk].

Not only were rich fabrics used but they were often decorated with other fabrics, gold embroidery, motifs and spangles (sequins) made of gold and silver, jewels and fringes. Mitres in particular were very richly embellished. The mitre donated to the Minster by Archbishop Thomas Rotherham is described in the inventory of *c.* 1500 as:

> *'una preciosissima et magna mitre cum duabus pendulis auro circumdatis et lapidibus preciosa, saphiris et rubeis'.*

Similarly there were copes and amices set with pearls:

'una capa rubia de tyssue cum le orfreys de perle'
'une amica de perles'.

Vestments might be made up of contrasting fabrics:

'j vestment de veridi damaske et orfra Cypri velvet'
'j vestment de rubio cum animalibus de auro & uno blodio orfra cum floribus'
'on vestment of blew velvet hemmyd wt cloth of gold'.

Embroidery was also used as a method of enriching the textiles:

'unus pannus pro altari brudatus'
'another reade cope of clothe of tishewe with orphry of needlework with the five wounds'
'a riche sudarye imbrothred with goulde'.

The motifs used, either embroidered or applied precious metals, were extremely varied and of a religious or secular nature: crowns, 'stellis de auro operatis' (stars of gold work), 'bestiis et floribus', 'skaloppes', 'gryffethes', 'squyrrelles', dragons, 'estrigefederes' (ostrich feathers), 'leonibus le rawmpyng de auro' (a ruddy lion rampant, in gold). Other designs were the arms of the donor's family such as those of John Pakenham, Treasurer of the Minster; of the Fitzhugh family and the arms of England. There were also various saints depicted; St. Andrew, St. Paul, St. Thomas and of course, St. Peter.

The records of the Minster with respect to the purchase of vestments are scant. In fact the Minster probably purchased few vestments. It is obvious from the inventories made over the years that many articles were donated by devout parishioners and clergy and in a few cases, royalty. The list of the possessions of the Chantry shrines quotes many examples of such gifts.

'j corporale de rubio velvet ex dono Willelmi Bordclever' [chantry at the altar of St. Jerome, 1510]
'unum vestimentum integrum de serico albo cum ij tuniculis et ij albis, ex dono domini Henrici de Ingilby' [altar of St. Mary the Virgin, c.1420]
'a cope of raised clothe of goulde, of the Lord Darcye's gift'
'unum vestimentum integrum de lecto dominae Philippae reginae . . . cum ij tuellis et frontells' [St. Mary the Virgin, c.1420]

This last refers to the gift of the bed hangings of Queen Philippa of Hainault, who married Edward III in York on 24 January 1328. The hangings were cut up and made into vestments and the record of the cost of the making up into thirteen copes, six tunicles and one chasuble is recorded in the Minster Fabric Rolls for 1371 as £17 2s. 11d. Previously Eleanor of Castile, the Queen of Edward I, donated her bed hangings to the Minster when she died in 1290 and the green cloth of gold fabric was made into one chasuble and four albs with embroidered apparel and amice.

The extent of the custom of donating a gift to the Church can be understood by reading wills of York citizens. Before the Reformation it was the custom for every individual to bequeath a gift to their Church or parish priest or to the Minster. This was known as the mortuary gift and its nature varied from place to place and on the social or religious status of the donor. In York, as in many other places, the tradition was to give 'my best gown'. The will (1512) of Lady Jane Harper, widow of John Harper, merchant and Lord Mayor of York states:

'And I bequeth for my cors presant my beste gowne after the maner and custome of the city of Yorke.'

Canons were required by the Dean and Chapter to donate a cope and palfrey (horse) of a certain value; this gift was known as the *mortuaria canonicorum*. In 1370 Canon David de Woolor bequeathed a cope of black velvet decorated with gold embroidery thickly set between with gold stars; another with a silver morse decorated with gilt with an image of the Blessed Mary surrounded by stones of coral, and £20 in lieu of a palfrey.

One of the richest gifts of vestments left to the Minster must surely be that of Bishop Skirlaw of Durham who died in 1405. To York Minster he left a suit of dark red velvet embroidered with gold crowns and stars, including one chasuble, four dalmatics/tunicles, six stoles, three maniples and three amices with embroidery, and three belts. There was also a frontal and sub-frontal for the altar, a cloth for the lectern and five copes with gold orphreys. This set of vestments was bought in London and cost 120 marks (£80) which would be in the region of £30,000 at present prices! Similar sets of vestments were also given to Beverley Minster, Wells Cathedral and Howden Minster and Norton, Darlington, Chester-le-Street and Bishop Auckland churches.

Although the Fabric Rolls of York Minster are scant and give little information on the source of the vestments, it is still possible to find out a little about the makers of vestments by consulting the Freemen's Register of York. Craftsmen were obliged to pay to be granted the right to practise their craft or trade, unless they lived in certain church property, the Liberties, and this purchase of the Freedom to trade was registered in the Civic records. Between 1394 and 1551 there were eighteen Vestmentmakers who registered as Freemen and in 1591 the 'Ordinances of the Companie of Imbroderers, Vestmentmakers, Cutters and Drawers' were drawn up. After 1551 no one became a Freeman Vestmentmaker – not when the Reformation had abolished most vestments. Instead, the craftsmen became Freemen Imbroiderers and one must presume that most of their work was secular.

The accumulation of treasures over hundreds of years was enormous, as is shown by the inventory of 1510 which listed mitres, croziers, brooches, phials, incense burners, sconces, basins, staves, hand warmers, salt cellars, paintings, morses, books, a unicorn's horn and other items. The vestments included seventy-one white copes, twenty-six black, seventy-six red, thirty-four green and seventy blue copes. Together with the chasubles, dalmatics and tunicles there were four hundred and seventy-five vestments!

The final great inventory of church goods may have been made in response to Edward VI's initiative, in 1549, of a Commission to make inventories of church treasures. Previous to this, some churches were reportedly selling off their holdings for the benefit of the parishioners rather than risk government seizure, bearing in mind what had happened to the monasteries and other religious foundations in the Acts of 1536 and 1539. In order to forestall further unofficial losses of church treasures, Edward required each church to produce an inventory of goods and the clergy were instructed to keep the treasures safe. This inventory records two hundred and thirty-one copes, thirty-six chasubles, six dalmatics and twenty tunicles, representing a loss of one hundred and eighty-two vestments from the previous inventory. It is not possible to know if the discrepancy is due to inaccurate accounting, natural wastage, unofficial disposal of the treasures or perhaps a combination of these. Despite the efforts of Edward, church goods continued to be sold off and in 1553, all the treasures were seized by a new Commission of the King. The valuables were taken to the King's Treasury, some goods were sold off locally and the plain linen was distributed to the poor. Each church was permitted to keep one or two bells and a chalice and priests were allowed to wear only surplices and albs. Careful records had been made of the early stages of the Dissolution of the Monasteries and it is known, for example, that Richard Gowthorpe, a York haberdasher, bought vestments valued at 34s. 4d. from the Commissioners who were responsible for the dissolution, in 1536, of the St. Andrew Priory just outside the city walls. Unfortunately nothing is known of the details of the dispersal of the Minster treasures.

The problem of storing this quantity of textiles, along with all the other treasures, must have been considerable. Some of the altar cloths, frontals, superfrontals and curtains would have been in regular use in the various parts of the church. Inventories record that rich cloths and carpets were hung in the choir and that there were silk, damask, figured satin, cloth of gold, velvet and worsted cushions along with carpets in 'the vestibule'. The tomb of Archbishop Richard Scrope in the north-east bay of the Lady Chapel was hung with rich cloths on which were attached offerings of gold, silver and precious stones.

Vestments which were not in use would have been stored in chests and almeries (cupboards). The inventory of c. 1550 lists the vestments according to their place of storage rather than their type: 'in the vestry', 'in the chamber above', 'in the great cheste in the inner house' and 'in the upper house'. The Minster still possesses the two large quadrant-shaped chests which were used for storing copes laid flat, hood down, the front edges being brought over to meet in the centre of the chest, thus minimising folds. These magnificent chests date from the third quarter of the 12th century (Fig. 4a) and the middle of the 13th century.

A further problem associated with the large collection of textiles was that of their upkeep. Fabrics are obviously much more fragile than the gold and silver treasures and their care was thus more time consuming. The Treasurer of the Minster was ultimately responsible for the maintenance of all the treasures as well as the building. Many of his duties were delegated to the sub-Treasurer and his subordinates. In the 14th century two vestry clerks were specifically responsible for the vestments; an early 15th century account shows that they were paid 20s. and a woman was paid 8s. for the laundry work.

There were regular Visitations of all churches

by the Dean and Chapter to inspect the state of the building and the furnishings, the way in which services were carried out and the manner in which the clergy and the parishioners behaved. The records of these Visitations show that the Minster and other city churches were not always conscientious about the upkeep of the buildings and their contents. There were some disputes as to whether the priest or the parishioners were responsible for the repairs. In 1472 one of the many complaints against the Vicars Choral in Bedern was that a chasuble and its associated ornaments were made, not of silk as they should have been, but of worsted and other cloth. The same year the vestments in St. Michael le Belfrey were described as worn and torn. In 1481 the 'parysh church of our Lady Bushophyll' was criticised because 'Ye sayd churchwardens doyth not wasse ye albs, alter cloyths and surplesses skarsly once in a year'.

Again in 1510 St. Michael le Belfrey was unsatisfactory for a number of reasons including: 'Item that almerys chistes ordeynd for the anorments hath no lokkes nor keys' and because John Randald had bequeathed a vestment of 'greyn sattan' to the altar but his executors had given a vestment of 'greyn tutt' (presumably some inferior cloth).

In 1519 there were numerous inadequacies listed for the Cathedral Church of St. Peter (The Minster):

'Item all the hangynes of ye where lyeth opynly in the presbitory, dogges pysses on thame, wax droppys of thame . . .'

'Item ye clothe y^t coverse ye reyredewse is of party colors, whiche is not honeste for straungers to luke upon'

'Item the vestiary, there is a chest full of suspent stuffe y^t will make parores, amettes, coshyns, & to amende many usuall thynges in ye where, & such as ye secunde formes weres nowe is all so torne whiche tha walde amend well for every day.'

'Item the amendynge of the dalmatykes for ye Advent & Septuagesym myghte be done wt a litile cost, whiche nowe mosters away & not occupied.'

In 1544/5 during the years of the Reformation, matters were no better:

'Item, that there be manye copes, vestmentes and other anournements of the said Churche in greate decaye'.

Towards the Present Day

An account of vestments and furnishings in the Minster after the Reformation must be based on very sparse references and records. As the decades passed, the church experienced many changes which embraced a short return to Roman Catholicism, Puritanism and the Commonwealth, the Oxford Movement and further changes taking place today. All these and other events affected both church furnishings and ecclesiastical dress and it is interesting to look at the effigies in the Minster which commemorate Archbishops of York from the mid-13th to the 19th centuries.

The earliest representation is that of Walter de Gray, d.1255, in Henry III's reign. The Purbeck marble figure on top of the tomb is probably a standard quarry item of statuary and is of a bishop, not an archbishop. Of much greater interest is the painted figure on the lid of the archbishop's coffin which came to light when the tomb was extensively restored in 1968. This painting is almost certainly an attempt to portray de Gray himself and he is shown wearing an alb with gold patterned apparel at the hem, tunicle edged or fringed with gold and with a central pillar orphrey, blue sleeved dalmatic, red chasuble edged with gold, apparelled amice, mitre and pallium in accordance with his rank. His hands are gloved and he carries a primatial cross.

A fine brass in St. Nicholas's Chapel commemorates William de Greenfield, d.1316. His full chasuble, folded back over the arms, is worn with an embroidered amice-apparel, pallium, maniple and mitre.

Archbishop Savage, d.1507 was active in the reign of Henry VII and his dress continues the late mediaeval style of chasuble, pallium, maniple and mitre but a hundred years later, after the Reformation, Matthew Hutton, d.1606, the last Elizabethan Archbishop of York is shown lying full-length, wearing *rochet*, *ruff*, *chimere* and four-cornered Canterbury cap. The *rochet*, was a white linen vestment similar to an alb but worn only by bishops and archbishops. The sleeves were full and gathered into a wrist band. The *ruff* was the stiff pleated neckband and the *chimere* was the sleeveless outer garment worn open in front by bishops and archbishops.

Tobias Matthew, born in the last years of Henry VIII's reign, lived on into that of Charles I and his effigy of 1628 shows him still affecting a ruff with the now usual chimere and scarf, and a close-fitting black cap. The delightfully named Accepted Frewen, d.1664, whose father is said to have been a Puritan, wears a black, square-topped cap adorned with a black bobble. The 17th century was dominated by Puritanism when all church adornments were kept to the minimum and it is therefore surprising to find that the next three archbishops are sculpted wearing mitres which it is unlikely that they would have done in office.

Archbishop Sterne, d.1685, is followed only a year later by John Dolben who, as a student, had been wounded at the battle of Marston Moor. Dolben is shown lying gracefully on his elbow whilst Thomas Lamplugh, d.1691, is standing in a commanding pose, bearded and moustached and carrying his pastoral staff. His statue and that of John Dolben are noted by Celia Fiennes in her diary in 1697: 'that was the Archbishop whose statue is in white marble and shepherd's crook; just by him is the Effigy of another Bishop laying along cut in stone, and by the aise and mien he looks more like a soldier or beau than a Bishop, and so it seems he was in humour.'

The only archbishop commemorated in the 18th century is John Sharp, d.1714, in Queen Anne's reign. He wears a mitre, chimere and scarf.

Two effigies from the 19th century are of Archbishop Vernon-Harcourt, d.1847, wearing preaching gown, *bands* and wig which was old-fashioned by the time of his death, and Archbishop Musgrave, d.1860, wearing, rochet, *cravat*, bands and scarf. Neither is shown with a mitre. (*Bands* were oblong pieces of white linen worn round the neck, and a *cravat* was a wide piece of white linen tied high round the neck.)

Copes do not appear in any of the memorials;

they are the principal vestments worn on ceremonial occasions.

Some records survive telling of the internal management of the Minster and it is said that at the beginning of Henry VIII's reign, the Minster was in a sad state of disrepair and neglect and was being run by the Dean and two or possibly three Canons Residentiary together with a diminishing number of Vicars Choral. In 1541 the great shrine of St. William behind the high altar had been destroyed and five years later Archbishop Holgate enjoined the utmost austerity in the worship in the Minster. The church was to be cleared of all monuments and images and scriptural texts were to be painted on the chancel walls. The accounts of the clerk of the works for 1556 included expenditure on altars, tabernacles and candlesticks. The Prayer Book of 1549 (Edward VI) had stipulated that at Mass the priest was to wear a 'white alb, plain with vestment or cope' and other ministers 'albs with tunicles'.

A few gifts of vestments were made in the reign of Catholic Queen Mary but the treasures of the Minister were never the same again. In other places it is known that vestments were either burnt or used for secular or religious purposes. 'Many private men's Parlours were hung with Altar Cloths, their Tables and Beds covered with Copes instead of Carpets and Coverlids.' Some of the vestments were bought by recusant families who used them in secret and illegal Roman Catholic worship. In North Yorkshire at Masham near Ripon, Robert Wyville, from a well-known recusant family, bought five sets of Mass vestments, two copes, several tunicles and dalmatics, six corporaxes, three burses, two sanctus bells and various frontals. This purchase not only occurred as late as 1595 but was even publicly recorded in the Churchwarden's Account Book.

Little is known about Minster vestments during the long reign of Elizabeth I but in 1603 the city presented the Minster with a canopy of cloth of gold and two gilt crowns in honour of a visit from James I. An inventory of 1616 highlights the meagre possessions of the Minster – no chasubles, dalmatics or tunicles but there were three copes, various altar cloths, curtains, canopies and cushions including 'Eleaven long cushions made of old vestments and copes'. The inventory consisted of a mere twenty-seven items, mostly of little value.

Charles I came to the throne in 1625 and in that year it is noted that, 'the Minster also recovered testamentary gifts of a "frontclothe"

and canopy to make good the seizures of the Royal Commissioners'. The following year Archbishop Richard Neile records that a fine of £1,000 was imposed by the High Commissioners at York, and it was granted by Charles I to the Minster for repairs, a new organ and the maintenance of a library keeper. Other acquisitions were two altar frontals and a large carpet richly ornamented. The King himself visited the Minster in 1633 and presented to the Dean and Chapter a fine Bible and prayer book covered in red velvet embellished with silver-gilt mounts. These are still preserved in the Minster Library.

William Laud was appointed Archbishop of Canterbury in 1632 and as a high ritualistic churchman, he stringently enforced the Canons (Church Regulations) of 1604 which decreed that at the time of Divine Service, the altar must be covered with a 'decent carpet of silk'. Carpet was a normal description of a table covering and the throw-over altar cloths were adapted from the rich table coverings of the day. The inventory of 1634 shows that the Minster had been enriched by these and other acquisitions.

The rise of Puritanism and the Commonwealth period profoundly affected the church and in York, the siege of 1644 culminated in the surrender of the city to the Roundhead General Fairfax. Fairfax lived in Yorkshire where he owned large estates and it was he who prevented the despoliation of the Minster and undoubtedly saved the priceless stained glass. Even so, by order of the Lord Mayor, plate and brass were sold and three copes removed.

John Evelyn visited the Minster in 1654 and saw the Bible and prayer book covered in crimson velvet which had been presented by Charles I. He also noted 'a gorgeous covering for the altar and pulpit'.

The sequestrators were still active after the Restoration of the Monarchy and in 1662 it is recorded that 'there were three copes taken away by the Committee – for the rest, cussions canopies, cloths, linen and silkes . . . are remaining in the Church'.

Archbishop Lamplugh (1688–91) was a considerable benefactor and his gifts included an antependium (frontal) of crimson velvet richly adorned with a deep fringe of gold, together with a velvet hanging for the back of the altar. He also gave three large tapestries for the same use. Celia Fiennes noted in her diary in 1697 that 'in the Minster there is the greatest curiosity for Windows I ever saw . . . there is a very good organ, the table

FIGURE 4A   *13th century cope chest.*

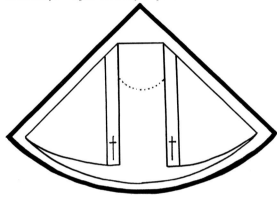

FIGURE 4B   *Diagram of a cope folded for storage.*

cloth and cuchions and books at the Communion table was crimson-velvet and hangings, and its embroyder'd very richly with gold of great depth and gold fringe at the bottom . . . The Embroydery at the table is almost a yard deep, that was given by Lamplue . . . I also saw the fine tissue canopy that was held over the head of King James the first when he came into England . . . then I saw a Chest that was triangular fashion the shape of the coapes when folded in the middle and so put into the Chest' (Figs 4a and 4b).

Some of the mediaeval hangings for the choir still survived together with one cope in the vestry in the late 17th century but in 1720 Dean Finch removed one of Archbishop Lamplugh's tapestries and the other two were removed by Dean Fountayne in 1761. In this year, two southern chapels in the South transept were 'tastefully refurbished with 16 yards of rich crimson Genoe velvet at 27/–

a yard which gave great satisfaction'. The same year and echoing a pre-Reformation custom, William Mason, Precentor, left to the church his surplice, cap, hood and scarf.

In the early 19th century, Archbishop Markham gave new velvet coverings for the High Altar, pulpit and throne and one must assume that other frontals were purchased in 1866 which did not meet with universal approval if the following extract from a letter written to the York Herald in October 1866 is accepted:

> . . . a fortnight ago the usual crimson cloth was removed from the communion table, and a green velvet one covered in front with white lilies was substituted. This I am told is one of four used by the ritualists, and has reference to the season of the year, and also to the Virgin Mary . . . This drew forth the plaudits of the ritualists, and was a source of deep sorrow to others. To the Archbishop, who, I understand, has no power in York Minster, it must be a source of great annoyance . . . who then, I would ask, is responsible for this folly?

Despite this broadside, a festal frontal and superfrontal for the High altar were presented by the Minster congregation in 1869 and it too had a lily amongst its symbols which certain people felt 'smacked of Popery'.

Cassocks and surplices were provided for the choristers in 1871, their previous habit having been coats trimmed with fur, introduced in about 1720.

The reintroduction of episcopal mitres was a slow and careful process. Copes had not been prohibited at the Reformation as they were a processional garment not a eucharistic vestment, but their use was not encouraged. Even in 1902 at the Coronation of Edward VII in Westminster Abbey, convocation robes were worn by the archbishops and bishops (chimere and scarf) but mitres with copes evidently came back into use in the Southern province shortly after this.

Dr Cosmo Gordon Lang, enthroned as Archbishop of York in January 1909 (and later to become Archbishop of Canterbury) recalls in his memoires that

> Some people expected that I would follow the London use and wear cope and mitre. But I deliberately did not do so, as I had no wish even to seem to play to any section within the Church. And there was a consequence of this worth

noting, of which I did not learn until long after. It seems that the clergy of Sheffield who were then almost wholly Evangelical, had been discussing the new Archbishop, about whom they had serious apprehensions, with the worthy Rural Dean, Gilmore. After the manner of the British Bishops on the advent of Augustine, they decided on a sign which would determine their opinion of what they might expect in the new *regime*. It was whether or not the new Archbishop would wear a mitre! As I did not, they were reassured; and from that time onwards the good Gilmore, distinguished by his long patriarchal whiskers, was my most devoted henchman, and all his clergy were most loyal and cordial.

Here I may add that later on quietly and without any fuss, first at an Ordination in the Minster, I wore cope and mitre, certainly the first to do so either there or in the whole Province of York since the Reformation. The custom was gradually extended and indeed welcomed, and I never had one single word of protest or remonstrance – an illustration, I think, of the wisdom of doing these things quietly and gradually . . . I lived to see vestments in ordinary use in the Minster, and again no word of protest ever reached me.

The Great Processional Banner was presented to the Minster in 1916 (Frontispiece and Figs 38–42) but the following year Dean Foxley Norris declared himself ashamed at the bareness of the Minster and set about making worship as grand as possible.

Copes were worn regularly in the Minster from 1923 and Eucharistic vestments followed soon after, following the gift of the magnificent Halifax High Mass vestments in 1925. Their first recorded use was on St. Peter's Day, June 1925, which was also a Thanksgiving and Commemoration of the Council of Nicaea sixteen hundred years before. The matching cloth of gold cope and mitre (Fig. 36) was worn by Archbishop Lang. A Solemn Eucharist was held in Westminster Abbey the same day and the correspondent of the *Church Times* of 3 July 1925 recorded the magnificent vestments of the representatives of the Greek and Russian Orthodox churches and went on to say 'Then came the English bishops in Convocation robes, a seemly and gentlemanly garb but singularly unimpressive. It was impossible not to regret that on this unparalleled morning, our bishops were not vested in cope and mitre.'

Slowly, new vestments and frontals have been acquired, some commissioned specially for the Minster, others as gifts or legacies and many, especially those of antiquarian interest, obtained through the good offices of Dean Milner White and the generosity of the Friends of York Minster.

The Minster Broderers' Guild was formed in 1966. It is a group of men and women who work in a voluntary capacity for the embellishment of the Minster in many forms of embroidery. The Guild is under the direction of a professional tutor, Jennifer Hall who trained at the Royal School of Needlework and projects are funded by the Dean and Chapter and the Friends of the Minster. It is hoped that standards of design and technical ability will carry on the fine traditions of the past.

Embroideries and Textiles in York Minster

Textiles from the tomb of Walter de Gray, Archbishop of York 1215–55

The tomb of Archbishop Walter de Gray in the South transept of the Minster was opened during extensive restoration work on the whole monument in 1968 and fragments of textiles were recovered. Of particular interest were the remains of a small cushion roughly 30 cm square under the Archbishop's head and two tablet-woven braids laid over his shoulders which could have formed the apparel of an amice or have been attached to a mitre.

The embroidered cushion fragments were in a tattered condition and all that remained was the gold and silk embroidery, the background material which was probably linen, having disintegrated completely. The design is a chequer pattern of square compartments containing motifs

FIGURE 5 *Design (reconstruction) on a cushion cover from the tomb of Archbishop Walter de Gray c.1255.*

which are repeated diagonally from upper left to lower right. This was a favoured pattern for cushions and is known from other survivals from the 13th century and on the tombs of King Henry III and Queen Eleanor in Westminster Abbey. Both the front and back of the cushion had four rows of compartments which contained motifs in stylised and angular manner; labyrinth patterns, plant and tree forms, doves with wings raised, peacocks, lions bearing cross staves and deer with branched antlers. All the bird and animal motifs are mediaeval symbols of the Resurrection (Fig. 5).

The background is worked in long-armed cross stitch with silk thread which originally might have been in contrasting colours (Fig. 6a).

Conservation of the cushion fragments together with one of the tablet-woven braids was carried out by Mrs Landi of the Victoria and Albert Museum; the second braid was conserved by Mr Baynes-Cope of the British Museum.

A set of kneelers, their designs based on the cushion motifs, were designed by Joan Freeman and worked by the Minster Broderers in 1987. These kneelers will be placed on either side of the

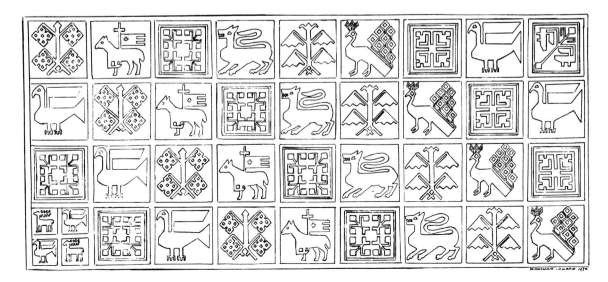

FIGURE 6A   *Fragment of cushion (detail) from the tomb of Walter de Gray c.1255.*

FIGURE 6B   *Canvaswork kneeler, the design based on the above, 1987.*

Archbishop's tomb, within a few feet of where the fragments were found. Stitches used include tent, mosaic, padded satin, backstitch and long-armed cross stitch (Fig. 6b).

Tablet-woven braids

Robert Patterson

The tablet-woven braids were examined at the same time as the cushion fragments and were described as 'highly skilled productions, uncommonly wide and woven with a large number of tablets'.

The right shoulder braid was in a fragmentary condition but the left one was reasonably complete and was examined again in 1983 for the purpose of weaving a facsimile. It measured 24cm long by 8cm wide and had been woven on 201 tablets, each with 4 holes, making a daunting total

of 804 warp threads in a width of 8cm! This was a record number of tablets in the 13th century and was not exceeded during the next four hundred years.

The threads are all silk, now faded to shades of brown, with traces of gold, but probably at one time of white, yellow, red or purple and metallic gold or silver-gilt. The reversing patterns of angular linear designs include diamond, swastika and key and are essentially weft designs (Fig. 7a).

The warp is arranged in red and yellow bands of very fine 2-ply silk, the same diameter as a single strand of 7-stranded embroidery silk (*Ver a Soie*), and is threaded through the tablets alternately left and right handed.

The weft is made of gold, red and white silk, similar to the warp, but used double throughout. The gold thread consists of an extremely fine metallic strip wound round a yellow silk core. This gold strip is only $\frac{1}{4}$mm wide, of slightly varying width and yet wound round the silk without a gap or overlap – that in itself must have been a prodigious feat.

During the weaving, the tablets are turned together one quarter turn and then two, sometimes three brocading wefts passed through the shed. The gold threads pass through the upper and lower warps as required, but the coloured ones pass only through the upper warps with appropriate tablets rotated a little further to provide single-thread tie-down points. The gold wefts are pulled tight but the coloured ones left loose and this produces a most unusual raised pattern (Fig. 7b).

The fragmentary right braid had exactly the same structure and format as the left and was probably a continuous length of eleven distinct patterns, with seven repeated in reverse and with four different cross-over designs (Fig. 8). This suggests a pattern sample or perhaps an apprentice piece. The fact that the tablets are turned in the same direction for at least 290 quarter turns implies a long warp to take up the resultant twisting and this further suggests a weaver at one end and a trainee at the other to produce a pattern sample and an apprentice piece simultaneously. This would also halve the weaving time and, as with the facsimile, it took four hours to weave a centimetre, any time-saving would have been most welcome.

The gold or gilt brocading wefts do not traverse the full width of the braid but leave a plain border at each side. This is the usual practice in early tablet-weaving but often the border has partially or completely disintegrated. This has

FIGURE 7A (above) *Tablet-woven braids from the tomb of Walter de Gray c.1255.*

FIGURE 7B (right) *Facsimile braid, 1983.*

been attributed to the cutting action of the metal-bound threads, but the decay of the second braid throws valuable new light on the subject. The progressive disintegration along the braid shows quite clearly that the plain sections between the patterns, as well as the borders, are the first to decay. These are the areas which contain no metal threads, indicating that it is the presence of gold or silver which preserves the silk, and its absence which permits decay, and that missing borders are not due to any cutting action of metallic threads.

Each braid has a strip of narrow braid, less than 1cm wide, sewn roughly across one end, and these have similar tablet-weave construction of alternating crosses and swastikas in red and gold, using 25 tablets and 100 silk warps (Fig. 8a).

It is presumed that the grave clothes were linen and not the customary silk as no trace remains of them. This, together with these sample braids with their roughly-sewn end braids, is probably explained by the circumstances of Archbishop de Gray's death in London in 1255 and his subsequent burial 200 miles away in York.

The facsimile wide braid was woven on a simple loom, now reduced in length for display purposes (Fig. 9), and a copy of the narrow braid has been incorporated in the mitre tails and stole of the vestments made for the present Archbishop of York, Dr John Habgood, so the braids of Walter de Gray live on (see pp. 58–9).

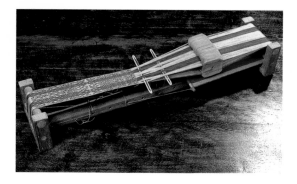

FIGURE 8 (right)   *Weaving patterns of the tablet-woven braids.*

FIGURE 9 (above)   *Simple tablet-weaving loom.*

FIGURE 10 (below)   *Crucifixion on the back of a chasuble, late 15th century.*

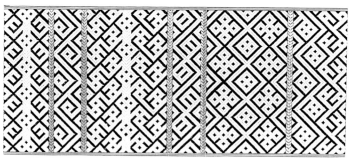

Crucifixion, late 15th century

This embroidery which adorns the back of a chasuble is probably North German, worked in Cologne.

The figure of Christ is surmounted by a scroll which may have had the letters INRI worked on it, the initial letters of the Latin words, *Jesus Nazarenus Rex Judaeorum*, Jesus of Nazareth, King of the Jews. At the top, God the Father stretches out his left hand in blessing; the orb in his right represents the world (Fig. 10).

The crucifix is shown as the green branches of a tree, not as cut timber and this is referred to in Luke xxiii 31 'If these things are done when the wood is green, what will happen when it is dry?'

To the left of the crucified Christ stands St. Peter with a key and book, on the right is St. Paul with a sword. At the foot of the cross are Mary, the Mother of Christ and St. John the 'beloved disciple'. Over their shoulders appear the heads of the two soldiers, Stephaton on the left and Longinus on the right, probably carrying a spear, but both figures have been cut down at some time.

At the foot of the cross stands a saint with a broad-bladed knife and small object in his other hand; this could be St. Bartholomew. The second figure, possibly holding a casket, might be St. Matthew.

A green crucifix may be seen in stained glass in a window in the North nave aisle, the Pilgrimage window, the same window which contains St. Peter shown in Figure 2.

Cross-shaped panel, c.1490–1520

Probably North German, this embroidery is worked on natural coloured, coarse, plain woven linen. The Virgin and Child are standing on a crescent moon which pierces the disc of the sun and they are surmounted by an angel holding a crown over the head of the Virgin. This interpretation symbolises the Virgin as Queen of Heaven and the aureole surrounding the main figures represents divinity.

The saints supporting the Virgin are, on the left, St. Barbara holding a tower with three windows (representing the Trinity) and a female saint with a cup, St. Lucy or St. Prudentia.

Below the Virgin, the saint on the left holding a single arrow could be either St. Ursula or St. Christina, on the right, holding a long pair of pincers, St. Agatha or St. Apollonia.

At the foot of the panel, the two saints have been cut short but on the left, apparently carrying an *aspergum* (holy water container) may be St. Martha who is usually shown with a dragon at her feet, now missing, and St. Mary Magdalene with a covered cup or alabaster box of ointment (Fig. 11).

The embroidery is worked in laid and couched floss silks with details such as the lines highlighting the rays of the aureole worked in thick brown wool.

The faces and hands are applied silk-satin with embroidered and painted detail. The satin is applied over a layer of linen and one of parchment. Purchased 1955.

FIGURE 11 *Virgin and Child standing on a moonbeam, c.1490–1520.*

Embroidered panel of the Last Supper, c.1530

This altar frontal, said to be Spanish c.1530 may be rather later in date. The top of the table is decorated with small bunches of cherries and the two donors of the frontal are shown kneeling in the foreground (Fig. 12). Purchased 1954.

Altar frontal and picture surround, Pater Noster Chapel, c.1620–30 and 1650–75

Appliqué on silk, probably Italian c.1620–30 this fine altar frontal which adorns the Pater Noster Chapel has applied silver thread, silks, cord and some raised work. It is possible that the central motif may be of a later date.

Above the altar, the picture is surrounded with Italian appliqué work c.1650–75, originally cloth of silver and silver-gilt on a red ground (Fig. 13). Given by the Revd and Mrs D. C. Stewart-Smith, 1948.

FIGURE 12 (above)   *Altar frontal, Spanish, the Last Supper, c.1530 or later.*

FIGURE 13 (below)   *Altar frontal c.1620–30 and picture surround c.1650–75, Italian.*

Annunciation banner, 1670

The central panel of the Virgin with the Archangel Gabriel was probably woven in North Germany as a cushion cover (Fig. 14). At the top centre is a monogram surmounted by a crown. The letters of VMAR refer to *Vierge Marie* (the Virgin Mary) and the crown symbolises the Virgin as Queen of Heaven. The text below the picture in Latin from the Vulgate is taken from the Book of Ecclesiasticus vi 31.

The date *ANNO 1670* appears in the upper corners. This is almost certainly the date of the original cartoon for the panel of which at least four other copies are known. These include two pairs, one of each pair being a mirror image so one can assume that the Minster panel originally had a mirror image. Whether the panels were woven in 1670 or later is not known.

The original cartoon may have been based on a picture in a mediaeval book of devotion. These were known in England as Primers but this kind of book was not exclusive to England in the Middle Ages. Their contents varied from place to place and they were originally hand-written and could be lavishly illustrated. One important ingredient of these mediaeval books was a set of simple daily offices for the use of the laity, additional to those found in the priest's breviary, and known as the Hours of the Blessed Virgin Mary. These Hours were frequently preceded by a picture of the Annunciation similar to the one on this panel.

FIGURE 14 *Annunciation banner, woven tapestry, ANNO 1670 (detail).*

The literal translation of the verse in Hebrew from Ecclesiasticus is 'An ornament of gold is wisdom's yoke, and her fetters a cord of blue' – this explains the fetters in the corners of the panel and the relationship of the picture to Wisdom. The purpose of the blue cord was to attach tassels, an Old Testament custom. God told Moses to instruct the Israelites to make tassels like flowers on their garments, and 'into this tassel you shall work a cord of blue, and whenever you see this blue thread or cord in the tassel, you shall remember all the Lord's commandments and obey them and not go your own wanton ways.' The cord of blue is therefore linked to the fetters which are themselves God's commandments. The picture is a graphic and pictorial command to be obedient to God's law.

The link between the Blessed Virgin Mary and Wisdom was well-known in the Middle Ages. Lessons from Ecclesiasticus on Feasts of the Blessed Virgin Mary were commonplace and references to Wisdom also occurred frequently in books of devotion. They are all linked with the Annunciation and the Incarnation.

The central panel of the banner is surrounded by tapestry of a much coarser weave. On the reverse side is the inscription 'Remember before God the donor of this Banner, Colonel William Henton Carver, D.L., M.P., J.P., 1868–1961: tireless servant of God and his Church, of his country and his fellow men.'

Chasuble, c.1680

Dating from the 3rd quarter of the 17th century, this chasuble, which is Italian or French, may be compared with the embroidery of a similar date in the Pater Noster Chapel (Fig. 13).

On a red satin ground, the applied decoration is in silver and gold with gold outlines. There is original gold lace round the edges of the chasuble, but short lengths of velvet strip and fringe are later repairs (Fig. 15).

FIGURE 15 *Chasuble, Italian or French, 3rd quarter 17th century.*

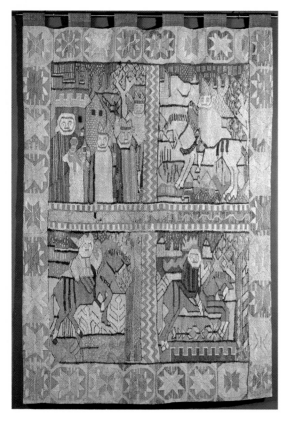

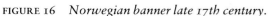

FIGURE 16   *Norwegian banner late 17th century.*   FIGURE 17   *The three Magi, 17th century.*

Norwegian banner, *c.*1685

Originally woven as a bedspread in rural Norway, this tapestry is now used as a banner and dates from the late 17th century. There are about 30 known tapestries similar to that in the Minster and they, together with another group which has the main figures framed by animals, are known as the 'Three Magi'. The three Magi have been transformed from the three wise men from the East, into three crowned princes of Norwegian mediaeval art (Fig. 16).

   European tradition calls them Caspar, Melchior and Balthasar and in this order they might represent old age, manhood and youth. They followed the star to Bethlehem 'and when they were come into the house, they saw the young child with Mary his mother, and fell down and worshipped him; and when they had opened their treasures, they presented unto him gifts, gold, frankincence and myrrh'.

   The Minster banner shows the same motifs as the tapestry in Figure 17 (which is in the Museum

of Applied Art in Oslo) but as a mirror image. The design is divided into four scenes separated by a right-angled cross. The three Magi mounted on their steeds have one panel each. They are crowned and wear ruffs, short jackets and wide breeches. Some details are clearer in Figure 17 but Balthasar is on the blue horse and the beardless figure traditionally represents youth. Melchior beside him can be identified by his short beard of manhood and above him, Caspar, old age, have arrived at their destination.

   In the fourth panel, the two older kings kneel (or stand) before Jesus while the youngest stands a little way behind the others. The Virgin is wearing a long, patterned gown and cloak. She wears a coifed head-dress appropriate to a married woman and the naked child sits on a linen cloth on her lap.

   In Figure 17 above the roofs and stars can be seen a faded date, slightly distorted, AD 1625. There is also an almost illegible inscription on the horizontal arms of the cross which seems likely to translate as 'Hither[?] came the three kings who come from Sheba in the East'. In Figure 16 neither date nor inscription appears, leading one to suppose that the Minster tapestry is a later, less accurate and reversed work, but even the older tapestry is likely to date from the latter half of the 17th century rather than 1625 which is probably the date of the original cartoon.

The weft of the tapestries is wool and the warp probably linen, although some Norwegian pieces are woven with a wool warp. Vegetable dyes have been used, most of them native to Norway, but many tapestries are now so faded that they give an entirely incorrect impression of their original colours which must have been really brilliant. Purchased 1956.

Burse, *c.*1700

The cream silk damask ground is probably Italian, 17th century, embroidered in coloured silks with hand-beaten silver strip used for the main decorations with additional coral beads and tassels. The central octagon shows the Virgin and Child. It is thought that the embroidery is either Greek or worked in a Greek community outside mainland Greece, 17th/18th century (Fig. 18).

FIGURE 19   *Gardner chasuble, Spanish or Portuguese, early 18th century.*

FIGURE 18   *Burse, Greek or Greek Community, 17th/18th century.*

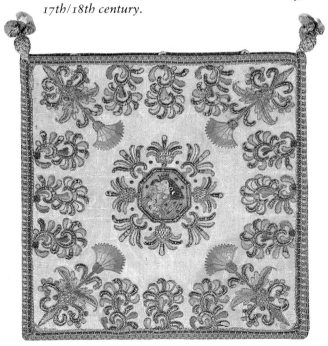

The Gardner chasuble, *c.*1700–50

The off-white silk background material is in a fragile condition but the coloured silk and metal thread embroidery is of very fine workmanship. Large mythical birds perch amongst scrolling foliage worked in long-and-short stitch, split stitch, Pekin knots, satin and stem stitch. The simulated braids are in couched gold thread worked in a chevron pattern. There is some padding, both stitched and over parchment and Italian couching on the gold leaves. The chasuble is thought to be Spanish or Portuguese, first half of the 18th century (Fig. 19). Given by Mrs Faith Gardner of Gray's Court, 1942.

Portuguese chasuble, *c.*1725–60

Rose-coloured silk decorated with flowers, birds, butterflies and insects in addition to a dove, the Virgin and Child, the Lamb and flag and cupids.

From the centre of some of the flowers on the central pillar orphrey rise tiny angels, some playing musical instruments . The design is almost symmetrical, flowers and birds balancing each other on either side, but on the right, in accordance with legend, a pelican feeds three chicks with drops of blood from her breast. On the left, this group is worked with a fourth chick hurrying to join the other three with wings raised and legs at full stretch.

Stitches include long and short, satin, stem, fly, fishbone, French knots and couched metal threads. The chasuble is thought to be Portuguese, c.1725–60 (Figs 20a, b and c).

FIGURE 20A (above) *Portuguese chasuble, 1725–60.*
FIGURES 20B and C (left) *Details from the Portuguese chasuble.*

Dossal, St. John's Chapel, c.1735–40

The embroidered green ribbed silk from which this dossal or hanging has been made was originally the skirt of a magnificent dress. The chinoiserie design is worked in floss silks in long and short stitch together with very fine Jap gold and silver, plate gold and thin gold wire twisted round a silk core. Stitched padding and padding over parchment are used. The embroidery is of very high quality using the same technique of shading, *points rentrés* as in contemporary woven silks.

The open front edges of the skirt of the dress are bordered with a scroll design in metal threads culminating in a vignette of a lady seated at the bottom of a long flight of steps. She has caught a huge fish with her bamboo rod and line, a fishing creel is by her side and a small crescent shaped

FIGURE 21 *Dossal in St. John's Chapel (detail) French, 1735–40.*

FIGURE 22 *Chasuble, cherub-with-a-dog design, French, 1735–40.*

boat is sailing out into the lake (Fig. 21). The main area of the material is decorated with scrolling foliage interspersed with six or seven repeating motifs which include a youth seated by a flowing stream, bouquets of flowers and fanciful turreted castles. The material is French, mid to late 1730s.

St. John's Chapel is the regimental chapel of the King's Own Yorkshire Light Infantry and the dress from which the dossal is made was purchased by the regiment in 1947 to mark a visit of the regiment's Colonel-in-Chief, Her Majesty Queen Elizabeth, now the Queen Mother. The dress silk has been paned with silk of a slightly later date.

Chasuble, cherub-with-a-dog, *c.*1735–40

French silk *c.*1735–40. The off-white tabby ground is brocaded in coloured silks and silver thread. The design is of the 1730s despite the use of *rocaille* (Fig. 22).

Cream taffeta Low Mass set, *c.*1745–50

Chasuble, stole, maniple, burse and veil of taffeta embroidered with scrolls in gold and flowers in coloured floss silks. The veil retains its original gold lace and the chasuble its braids and pink, glazed linen lining. The embroidery is worked in long and short stitch, stem and French knots together with gold threads. French, *c.*1745–50 (Fig. 23).

English silk Low Mass set, *c.*1760–65

Chasuble, stole, burse and veil of brocaded English silk, *c.*1760–65. The white ground is ribbed and woven with a satin stripe. The design is brocaded in gold thread, red silk and chenille and the material is typical dress silk (Fig. 24). Given by the Revd E. J. G. Forse, 1943.

FIGURE 23   *Chasuble, French, c.1745–50.*

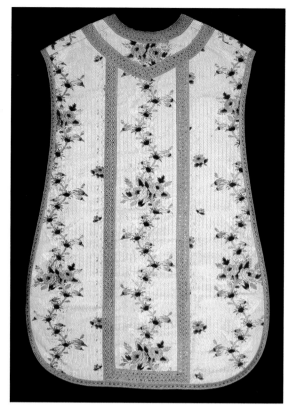

FIGURE 24   *Chasuble, English, c.1760–65.*

FIGURE 25   *Chasuble (detail) English, c.1765–70.*

English silk Low Mass set, c.1765–70

Chasuble, stole, burse and veil of white silk damask brocaded in coloured silks, *c.1765–70*. This low mass set has been re-made from a dress and signs of pleats remain from a sack-back (Fig. 25).

The Secker cope, 1760

Made for Dr Thomas Secker, Archbishop of Canterbury 1758–68, on the occasion of the coronation of George III in 1760.

The cope is of claret-coloured silk with a woven repetitive design of small flowers in ogival framing of leafy stems. There is no embroidery and the hood is flat. This kind of silk was normally used for men's wear in that period.

The cope has been extensively cleaned and conserved by the Textile Conservation Centre in Hampton Court.

FIGURE 27 *Dalmatic, French (Lyons) 3rd quarter 18th century.*

FIGURE 26A (above) *The Secker cope, c.1760.*
FIGURE 26B (below) *Detail of the Secker cope.*

The cope was given to York Minster in 1917 by a descendant of the Archbishop, the Revd John C. Gawthorne, Vicar of Edstone, Yorkshire.

Thomas Secker was born at Sibthorpe, Nottinghamshire in 1693 and it is said that 'the Archbishop left no family, but the late Revd Secker Gawthorne of Car Colston, Nottinghamshire has in his possession a fine portrait of the Archbishop together with his seal, gold snuff-box and a miniature portrait of King George III given to the Archbishop by the King whom he had baptised, confirmed and married' (Figs 26a and b).

Dalmatic, c.1750–75

French silk, third quarter of 18th century, *ornemen d'eglise*. This type of silk was never used for fashionable ladies' dress and the styles changed more slowly. One constant feature is the point repeat used when normal fashionable silks had straight repeats. This is a good, typical example and such silks were an important part of Lyons production (Fig. 27). Given by Charles van der Heyden, 1987.

Chinese silk Low Mass set, c.1830 and 1948

This set of vestments has a fascinating history recorded by Dean Eric Milner-White in the

Annual Report of the Friends of the Minster in 1947 (Fig. 28).

The previous year, Dean Milner-White had been captivated by the colour and woven decoration of two pieces of Chinese silk which HM Queen Mary had loaned for display at the Royal School of Needlework. The Dean wrote to Queen Mary after the exhibition and asked if he might have the pieces of silk for use in York Minster.

Her Majesty most graciously consented to this request, provided that the sum of £5 per piece be given to the Royal Naval Benevolent Trust. After carrying out this proviso, the pieces of silk were made up into two burses and two veils. It transpired that the material was fragments left over from a length of Chinese silk which the Emperor of China had given to Queen Victoria as a wedding present in 1837. It was made up into hangings for the Queen's bed-chamber, including her four-poster bed. About 1867 the suite mysteriously disappeared from Buckingham Palace and was subsequently included in a public auction.

Shortly afterwards the disappearance was discovered and enquiries were made. Sir Henry Ponsonby, Private Secretary to Her Majesty, traced the purchase to a Mr George Prince of Prince's Club who at once agreed that the material must be returned to the Palace. Her Majesty, however, graciously intimated that Mr Prince should retain part of the fabric as a souvenir and later on, this part came into the possession of Queen Mary and thence into the care of the Minster.

Dean Milner-White was anxious to match the colour of the burses and veils with sufficient silk to make a chasuble and stole and enlisted the help of Mr Keith Murray of Messrs Watts & Co., London who had been of invaluable help to the Minster over the years.

Mr Murray was unable to help from his own firm's stock, but told the Dean that Liberty's had just received a delivery of silks from China for which they had scoured the country. The Dean and Mr Murray set off for Liberty's with one of the veils; as soon as the veil was displayed the head of the department exclaimed that it posed no problem as they had a length of almost identical silk newly arrived from the East! This length of silk brought from China in 1948 was a remarkable match with that which had been woven in about 1830 and chosen by the Emperor of China for his wedding present to Queen Victoria in 1837. The woven design was on a slightly smaller scale, but it was an extraordinary coincidence after so many

FIGURE 28　*Low Mass set, the Emperor of China's wedding present to Queen Victoria, c.1830 also 1948.*

years, and a chasuble, stole and maniple were made from this silk to complete the low mass set as originally envisaged.

Altar frontal, St. Stephen's Chapel, c.1856

Two pieces of sea-green, heavy ribbed silk with an all-over design of small flowers have been joined together to form this frontal. The silk is Chinese, c.1820–50 in that the embroidery silks show no signs of aniline dyes which were first used in 1856. The flowers are worked in satin stitch, French knots, stem stitch and couched gold threads. The altar was formerly the high altar in the Choir sanctuary and the fine painted, terracotta Calvary altarpiece together with two wings, presently in store, were designed by A. G. Street in 1879 (Fig. 29).

Hangings in the Archbishop's throne (choir), *c.*1860

Three panels of crimson velvet with a leaf pattern in silver-gilt thread on cut and uncut pile. The material had originally been made up into two dalmatics which had been sent from Russia for sale in England. The dalmatics were bought by the Friends of the Minster in 1944 and the material re-used to form the hangings. The velvet could be either Russian or French, *c.*1860 (Fig. 30).

Choir pulpit hangings, 19th century

Three panels of 'Hampton Court' velvet, the design in brown and light red on white, voided satin ground, 19th century reproduction. This fine quality velvet is based on the design of the hangings which were commissioned for Queen Anne's state bed in 1714. Queen Anne died before the bed and other chairs and stools for the Royal bedchamber were completed, but they may still be seen at Hampton Court Palace.

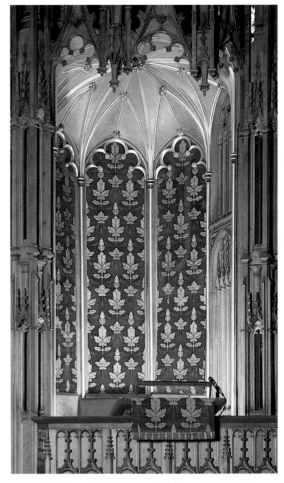

FIGURE 29 (below)   *Altar frontal, St. Stephen's Chapel, Chinese, mid 19th century.*

FIGURE 30 (right)   *Hangings in the Archbishop's throne, Russian or French, c.1860.*

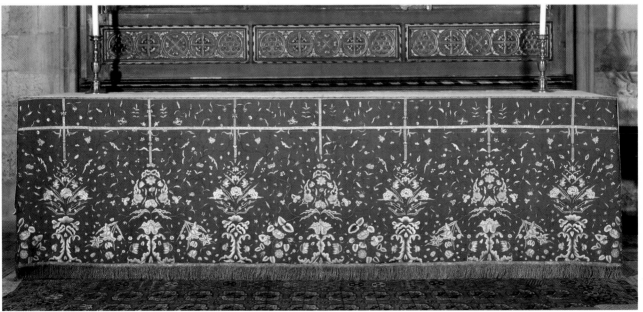

Festal frontal, High Altar, 1869

This frontal, designed by the architect John Sedding and worked by 'the ladies of St. Margaret's House, East Grinstead' (the Society of St. Margaret) was presented to the Dean and Chapter of York by the Minster's congregation in 1869. A contemporary photograph (Fig. 31) shows the High Altar at Christmastide 1869 and records a number of interesting details.

On the centre of the altar is a 150cm wooden cross covered with evergreens and white flowers. Plants of the aspidistra type have their pots swathed in moss and ivy and swags of evergreens hang behind and above the altar. The pair of silver pricket candlesticks do not contain candles for, since the Reformation, altar furnishings had been kept to the minimum and the use of ornaments severely curtailed. Following the lead of the Oxford Movement usages were becoming more relaxed but churches were accused of Popish practices when they made changes too quickly. Candlesticks first returned to altars without candles, slowly the addition of candles was accepted but they were not lit. Finally the change was completed by the lighting of the candles and

FIGURE 31 (above)   *High Altar festal frontal, 1869.*

FIGURE 32 (right)   *Right-hand panel (detail) of High Altar festal frontal.*

the addition of floral decorations of a sombre kind typical of the Victorian age.

It is interesting to note that the frontal, which is approaching 120 years of age, shows no wear at the centre front. This is because in 1869 and in some churches until quite recently, the celebrant stood at the North end of the altar in accordance with the Church Rubrics of 1662, therefore there was no rubbing against the front as happens today.

The frontal is divided into five panels and the significance of the design is partly explained in a York Chapter Act passed on 7 April 1869. In the centre St. Peter, patron saint of the Minster, holds the keys (the power of the Church) in his left hand whilst with his right he blesses the Minster.

To the left and right are the red rose, symbol of St. John, the beloved disciple and the white lily, emblem of purity and the Blessed Virgin.

The end panels are symbolic of the paradise of God; butterflies are emblematic of the resurrection and doves are emblems of peace (Fig. 32).

'Four dragons retreating to the North side'
appear in the end panels as four blue lions, each
bearing a scroll in his jaws inscribed *mors* (death).
As there is no documentary evidence of the artist's
thoughts, one can only make an informed guess
as to their significance, but as the general theme
of the frontal is about Life and Resurrection, the
following explanation is reasonable.

From the 5th century onwards in Christian
iconography, the lion was used as a type or pattern
of God in the redemption of His chosen people,
Israel. In the Middle Ages a series of books on
animals and their symbolism known as the
Bestiaries appeared and these were full of fact and
fanciful fiction, but the symbol of the lion as the
one who overcomes death and gives life persisted.
There is a delightful account which stated that
when a lioness brought forth a cub, it was born
dead; she would then watch over it for three days,
until the father lion arrived; he would breathe on
the dead cub and bring it to life. So God raised
Jesus from the dead on the third day.

This explanation fits the theme of the frontal
in that the four lions are a symbol of the new life,
and in each case they are devouring an inscription
with the word *Mors* (Death) written on it. All four
lions face North (left) but from early times the
North was always regarded as the mysterious and
deadly region where the Gospel needed to be
preached. This is a heritage of a time when
Christianity was centred around the Mediter-
ranean. The place for missionaries to go and
preach the Gospel was northwards into Europe.
It was a relic of this idea which has persisted down
to our own day, and still happens – where at the
eucharist, clergymen read the Epistle from the
South side, but always read the Gospel from the
North side of the altar. It was once true that it
was to the North that the Gospel needed to be
preached and the symbolism has stuck.

The right-hand panel (Fig. 32) bears the
embroidered date AD 1869 and an orb and cross,
an early version of the St. Margaret's convent
emblem.

The superfrontal is adorned with eight angels
playing musical instruments interspersed with five
shields bearing the arms of the See of York, King
Edwin (who founded the first cathedral), Archbishop Thoresby (who built the choir), Archbishop Wilfrid (who restored the cathedral), and
the arms of the Chapter of York. This heraldry
is interesting and characteristic of the revival of
interest in heraldry which was just beginning.
Unfortunately there are a number of inaccuracies

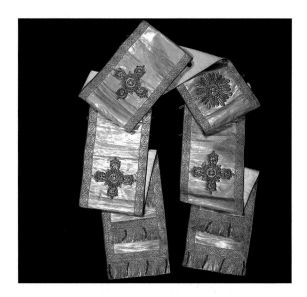

FIGURE 33A   *Omophoriun, Russian, c.1898.*

FIGURE 33B   *Detail of the omophoriun.*

especially with the tinctures (colours) and it is also
unusual to find the Ancient arms of the See of York
impaling those of the modern See. The crossed
keys are the attributed arms of St. Peter, not of
the Chapter which has never had arms of its own.

The background material is cream silk damask
and the embroidery includes appliqué, laid gold
threads, laid cords and heavy padding together
with long and short stitch, chain, stemstitch and
iridescent beetles' wings.

The Sister who began the embroidery work-
shop at St. Margaret's Convent in a very small
way, *c.*1865, was Sister Isa, Isabella Ann Sedding.

Omophoriun, *c.*1898

An omophoriun is the Russian Orthodox Church's equivalent of the pallium (see p. 62) in the Western Church, and is worn by bishops and archbishops.

The omophoriun illustrated is 390cm long and 30cm wide. It is worn passed loosely round the shoulders, one end hanging down in the middle of the front and the other in the middle of the back. It is then secured at its intersections with buttons and loops to keep it in place.

Made of cloth of silver, the motifs are all applied. Each is heavily padded and appears to be made from two parallel pieces of string covered with closely-wound plate gold or alternatively, very narrow gold braid; the covered string is then twisted to form the required shapes. Smaller shapes also wound with gold plate or braid form the lesser details which are firmly stitched into place before the completed motif is appliquéd on to the vestment. The whole length is outlined with gold braid and finished at the ends with two rows of gold bullion fringe. The buttons are filigree gold (Figs 33a and b).

This omophoriun was presented to Archbishop William MacLagan by the Archbishop of Smolensk during a visit to Russia in 1897.

Chalice veil, *c.*1900

Worked on cream satin in floss silks, couched gold and silver threads and sequins, this embroidered panel is Chinese, *c.*1900, and produced for the Western market (Fig. 34).

FIGURE 34 (below left)   *Chalice veil, Chinese export, c.1900.*
FIGURE 35 (above)   *Five stoles, English, late 19th–early 20th century.*

Stoles, *c.*1875–1910

Five stoles from the last quarter of the 19th century and up to about 1910 (Fig. 35).

The Halifax High Mass vestments, *c.*1909

This set of vestments includes a cope and mitre and was given to the second Viscount Halifax (d.1934) in 1909 as part of a presentation to mark the Golden Jubilee of the English Church Union and Lord Halifax's 41st year as its President; 1,400 members had subscribed to the gift.

Lord Halifax presented the vestments to York Minster in 1924 and it is recorded that they were first worn on St. Peter's Day, 1925, with the Archbishop (Dr Cosmo Gordon Lang) wearing the cope and mitre (Fig. 36).

The vestments are of cloth of gold with orphreys outlined in red and gold braid, the hems finished with red and gold fringes. The hood of the cope bears the sacred monogram (IHS) surrounded by an aureole worked in *or nué*, and the set is lined with blue silk twill. It is thought that the vestments may have been made in Belgium.

FIGURE 36   *Halifax High Mass vestments c.1909.*

St. Hilda's banner, *c.1912*

Designed by Sir Ninian Comper and worked by the Wantage Sisters, the banner was commissioned for the Church Congress held in Middlesbrough in 1912 (Fig. 37).

St. Hilda, holding Whitby Abbey, is superimposed on the arms of Robert de Brus II (or a saltire and chief gules). Prominence is given to de Brus because the manor of Skelton-in-Cleveland was given to his father Robert de Brus at the Norman Conquest. De Brus II founded Guisborough Priory on the family land in about AD 1120 and he also gave the site of the future St. Hilda's church in Middlesbrough 'together with immense possessions' to Whitby Abbey. The Abbey founded a Benedictine cell on the Middlesbrough site where St. Hilda's church was eventually built, only to be demolished in 1969.

The arms at the bottom left are those of the See of York impaling Lang (Archbishop Cosmo Gordon Lang, 1909–28) whilst those on the right are the arms of Middlesbrough (which has been given the ancient spelling on the banner). The scroll above St. Hilda reads, 'One generation shall praise thy works unto another and declare thy power'. Appliqué with couched gold threads.

The Great Processional Banner, *c.1914–16*

The banner measures 2.85m from the cross-bar to the bottom of the tasselled shields and 1.35m in width.

There is no record in contemporary Chapter minutes referring to the banner but a report in the Yorkshire Gazette for Saturday, 22 April 1916 states that, 'Tomorrow [Easter Day] a very beautiful banner will be presented to York Minster by a layman'. This benefactor was C. M. Forbes, Land Agent to the Dean and Chapter from 1886–1926.

Designed by W. J. (later Sir Walter) Tapper, architect and adviser to the Dean and Chapter from 1908–35, from cartoons by the stained glass artist John Charles Bewsey, the work was carried out by Messrs Watts & Co., London.

FIGURE 37   *St. Hilda's banner 1912.*

FIGURE 38 *The Great Processional Banner (reverse)* c.1914–16.

FIGURE 39 *Pelican and chicks (detail) from the Great Processional Banner.*

On one side of the banner is Christ crucified flanked by St. Mary, mother of Christ, and St. John, the youngest Apostle, traditionally portrayed as cleanshaven. (Fig. 38). A wide border of trailing stems and flowers is interspersed by symbols of the Passion and at the top centre, a pelican with six chicks (Fig. 39). Legend says that the pelican has the greatest love of all creatures for its offspring which it feeds with drops of blood from its own breast. This legend led to the pelican symbolising Christ's sacrifice on the Cross for the sake of all mankind.

The shields at the bottom of the banner bear the sacred monogram, IHS, the arms of the City of York and of the Diocese of York.

The front of the banner shows Christ in Majesty handing the keys to St. Peter to whom the Minster is dedicated (Fig. 40 and Frontispiece). The West front of the Minster appears in the bottom right-hand corner (Fig. 41).

The wide border enclosing the central panel bears Our Lord's charge to St. Peter in Latin which in translation reads, 'I say to you that you are Peter and on this rock will I build my Church' (Matthew xvi 18). In the corners of the border are the heads of the great Northern prelates, St. Wilfrid, St. Aidan, St. Cuthbert and St. Columba. On the pendant shields are the sacred monogram and the ancient and modern arms of the See of York.

The background material of the banner is rose-red silk damask with applied velvets, plain silks and damasks. The embroidery includes laid gold threads, long and short stitch, split stitch and stem stitch in floss silks. The head of Christ (Frontispiece) shows the superb working of the face, hair, beard and crown. The banner is, without doubt, one of the finest examples of Church embroidery of its date in this country.

In 1983, the Friends of the Minster sponsored the complete restoration of the banner and it was returned to Messrs Watts in London. The firm was

FIGURE 40
*The Great
Processional
Banner (front).*

FIGURE 41 *West front of the Minster (detail) from the Great Processional Banner.*

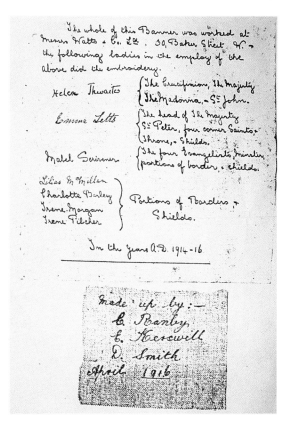

FIGURE 42 *Linen notice from inside the banner.*

most interested in being able to work on this large and important embroidery which had left their workrooms sixty-seven years previously. On separating the front of the banner from the back, a piece of linen was found sewn inside with the signatures of the embroideresses who had been involved in its making, together with those of the three people who had made it up (Fig. 42). A second label was added to the first, recording the restoration work completed in 1984.

Barely six weeks after the return of the banner to the Minster, the South Transept in which it was kept was devastated by fire. Although the oak and glass banner case was black, wet and covered in debris, the banner itself was unscathed.

Altar frontal, St. Nicholas's Chapel, *c.*1920

Nicholas is said to have been Bishop of Myra in Asia Minor in the first half of the fourth century AD. A number of spectacular acts and miracles have been accredited to this saint and some of them are recalled in the design of this altar frontal.

Eight of the Northern Saints flank St. Nicholas including (left) the Venerable Bede holding a book and quill and (third from the right) St. Cuthbert carrying the head of St. Oswald. The head had been taken to Lindisfarne for burial and then, when threatened by a Danish invasion, it was placed in the coffin of St. Cuthbert and eventually, after much travel, it was taken to Durham which was its final resting place.

St. Nicholas is shown with a book on which rest three money bags. This refers to the legend of the poor family with three young daughters for whom the parents could raise no dowries. Bishop Nicholas heard of their plight and one night he placed three bags of money inside their window without being seen, so that the girls were provided for. Eventually, over the centuries, the three money bags were adapted into the three gold balls of the pawnbrokers' sign and Nicholas is their patron saint (Fig. 43). Nicholas is also the patron saint of children (as Santa Claus), sailors and merchants.

The superfrontal, is embroidered with six small pictures recalling some of the wondrous acts in the legendary life of St. Nicholas. On the far left is depicted the scene when Nicholas as a new-born babe stood up in his bathtub for one hour quite unaided, whilst his mother and her two tiring women look on in astonishment (Fig. 44a). The fourth picture tells of the time when there was a famine in the land; two travellers arrived at an inn and asked for a meal, but the inn-keeper had no meat to offer them. He went out into the town and abducted three boys, murdered them and salted them down in a pickle barrel. Nicholas discovered the bodies in the brine cask and by making the sign of the cross over them, restored them to life. The guests look on whilst the inn-keeper leaves the room in haste (Fig. 44b).

The frontal, made in 1920 by Messrs Watts & Co., London, was presented to the Minster in memory of Dr Jalland by his widow. Restored in 1978 by the Minster Broderers.

St. Peter's cope, 1921

The present red silk damask cope replaces the original of red and gold brocatelle but the orphreys and hood were transferred from the previous cope. The hood bears the figure of St. Peter with a key, worked in couched gold thread, and partly in *or nué*. The face and hands are in floss silk using long and short stitch. The cope was presented to the Minster in 1921 by Mr Hoyland 'a Lancashire churchman', designed by Mr (later Sir Ninian) Comper and worked by the Sisters of Bethany (Fig. 45).

FIGURE 43 (below)   *St. Nicholas's altar frontal, c.1920.*

FIGURES 44A & B (right)   *Details from the superfrontal.*

The Southbourne vestments and St. Katharine's Embroidery Guild

In 1943, Dean Milner-White received a most generous gift of vestments from the Revd Edward John George Forse, who was Vicar of St. Katharine's Church, Southbourne, near Bournemouth from 1911–35.

In 1910 the St. Katharine's Embroidery Guild had been started at Southbourne by Miss Helen Barker who had trained in embroidery with the Wantage Sisters. The Guild was in being for fifteen years until Miss Barker died in 1925. In that time no fewer than eighteen Mass sets together with altar frontals, banners, albs and fair linen had been completed.

Father Forse had been actively involved in the design of many of the vestments, the detailed drawings for which had been done by Miss Edith Barker whilst her sister Helen supervised and instructed the embroiderers as well as doing much of the work herself.

High Mass sets in all the liturgical colours together with 'the most magnificent cope in the South of England' remain at Southbourne, but York Minster received nine Low Mass sets together with four albs lavishly decorated, corporals and palls in fine lacework. Some of the vestments were remade from old materials (see Fig. 24) and one set is listed as 'Spanish red, salvaged from a submerged vessel before 1900'.

Father Forse is still remembered with great affection in the parish of Southbourne and it is related that he was a great character. 'Forse by name and force by nature' he would declaim from the pulpit! He was a frequent preacher in London and Southwark, especially for the English Church Union and he wrote a number of books including *Ceremonial Curiosities and Queer Sights in Foreign Churches* which is a fascinating collection of anecdotes about his holidays on foot all over Europe from about 1905–26.

Much of this information is taken from another of Father Forse's books, *Fifty years of Southbourne Parish, 1876–1926*.

The Forse Stole, c.1925

A stole in the possession of the Archbishops of York at Bishopthorpe Palace records by heraldic means, the dioceses and colleges which figured in the life of Father Forse (Fig. 46). On the left appear the arms of the Bishopric of Lichfield where he attended Theological College; the Bishopric of Durham, ordained Deacon, curacies at Jarrow and Monk Wearmouth; Bishopric of Winchester, Vicar of St. Katharine's, Southbourne and Trinity College, Cambridge where he obtained his BA. On the right are shown the arms of the University of London, BA and MA (History); Bishopric of Southwark, Master of St. Saviour's College; Bishopric of Oxford, Curacies at Maidenhead and Guildford and University of Cambridge, MA. The stole is finely worked in laid gold threads and silks and is almost certainly by the St. Katharine's Embroidery Guild.

Other vestments received from Father Forse include the Melchisadec Low Mass Set, the Requiem Low Mass Set, the St. Peter and St. Paul Low Mass Set, and the Benedicite Low Mass Set.

FIGURE 45   *Hood from St. Peter's cope (detail) c.1921.*

FIGURE 46 (above)   *Stole, the Revd E. J. G. Forse, c.1925.*
FIGURE 47 (right)   *Melchisadec chasuble, c.1920.*

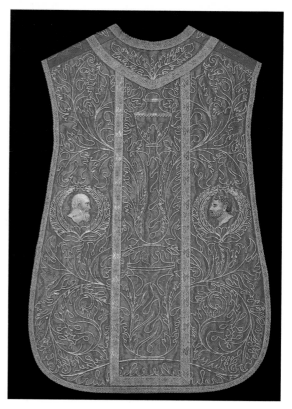

FIGURE 48   *Requiem chasuble, c.1920.*

FIGURE 49   *St. Peter and St. Paul chasuble,*
c.1920.

Melchisadec Low Mass set, *c.*1920

The embroidered orphreys are mounted on gold
silk, continental, the design based on an original
Byzantine silk, *c.*1000. The design of 'God the
Father enthroned and Blessing' is based on the
central top panel of the great altarpiece in the
cathedral of St. Bavon, Ghent, by Hubert van
Eyck and his more famous brother Jan van Eyck.
The panel of God the Father is one of the few
known works by Hubert van Eyck. The altarpiece
is now in the cathedral baptistry.

The Latin text surrounding the central panel
of the embroidery is translated, 'We have such a
high priest, who is seated at the right-hand of the
throne of the Majesty in heaven' (Hebrews viii 1).
On the halos of the two angels the Latin translates
'He took not on him the nature of angels . . . but
he took on him the seed of Abraham' (Hebrews
ii 16).

The embroidery is mostly worked in *or nué*
with heavy use of jewels. The faces and hands are
split stitch and the central panel and the two
angels have been worked separately and applied
to the background material, *c.*1920 (Fig. 47).

Requiem Low Mass set, *c.*1920

Blue-black silk velvet with the design in couched
silver threads outlined with silver cords. The
design recalls Christ's five wounds at the Crucifixion and represents Everlasting life (centre) surrounded by Wisdom, Mercy, Grace of God and
Consolation, *c.*1920 (Fig. 48).

St. Peter and St. Paul Low Mass set, *c.*1920

Italian or Spanish rose coloured silk damask, 19th
century. The design is worked in couched gold
threads in an outline pattern. The heads are in split
stitch using filofloss silks, *c.*1920 (Fig. 49).

Benedicite Low Mass set, *c.*1920

Green silk damask embroidered in couched gold
threads. The design of the set is based on the can-
ticle, *Benedicite Omnia Opera* (All ye works of the
Lord, bless ye the Lord) and about fifty 'works of
the Lord' are shown on the chasuble, stole, burse,
veil and maniple. A wealth of birds, beasts, reptiles
and insects set in leafy scrolls include delightful
humorous touches such as the spider in its web
and the tiny caterpillar no more than 3cm in length

FIGURE 50A *Benedicite chasuble, c.1920.*

FIGURE 50B *Detail from the Benedicite chasuble.*

humping its way up a leafy stalk (Fig. 50b).

Some of the animals which are heavily padded have been worked separately and applied to the damask, others are embroidered directly on to the background. There is some *or nué*, coloured metal threads and silver net overlay, especially on the wings of butterflies (Fig. 50a).

The German cope, 1946

Made of white and silver brocade, the orphreys and a wide band round the hem of the cope bear the following texts, 'Glory to God in the highest and on earth, peace, goodwill towards men' (Luke ii 14). 'All the ends of the earth have seen the salvation of our God' (Psalm xcviii 3) and 'The word was made flesh and dwelt amongst us and we beheld his glory' (John i 14) (Fig. 51). The hood carries a representation of the Nativity (Fig. 52).

Designed by Eric Klahn (1903–78) of Celle, West Germany, the embroidery was carried out by Liselotte Wedekind of the Werkstatt, Langhingen bei Wienhausen. The work is on fairly coarsely woven linen in hand-spun and dyed wools from the Werkstatt and the technique is *Klosterstitch* (Cloisterstitch).

The cope was made in 1946 for the Very Revd T. L. Weatherhead who was at that time serving as a RAF Chaplain with the British Forces of Occupation in Germany. In the early days after

FIGURE 51 *The German cope,* c.1946.

FIGURE 52   *Hood from the German cope.*

FIGURE 53   *Original design for the hood, Eric Klahn, c.1946.*

the war, trade by barter was not unusual and tobacco was a much-valued commodity. On the rear wall of the stable in the Nativity scene on the hood, appear two tobacco leaves; a reminder that this very cope had been paid for in this 'currency'.

When the then Squadron Leader Weatherhead was posted back to England, Eric Klahn was not too happy at the thought of his work leaving Germany. On reflection, however, he decided that perhaps it would be an act of reconciliation if the work of a German artist were to be more widely seen.

In later years, Father Weatherhead became Dean of Nassau in the Bahamas and in his retirement, offered the cope to York Minster in 1984. Unfortunately Eric Klahn had died in 1978, but his widow Äbtissin Barbara Bosse-Klahn was told of the present whereabouts of her late husband's work and was kind enough to offer the original design for the Nativity for inclusion in this book (Fig. 53).

Festal throw (Laudian) – Nave Altar, 1970

In 1970 the Yorkshire Federation of Women's Institutes made a most generous gift to the Minster to mark the Federation's Golden Jubilee. This took the form of a Festal throw-over cloth for the Nave altar, more correctly called a Laudian fron-

tal. About fifty Women's Institute members had spent over 10,000 hours during the previous five years embroidering the cloth in laid gold threads, gold kid, cords, coral silk and jewels. The design for the cloth, which is embroidered on both the front and back and the two ends, was by Joan Freeman of Harpenden, Hertfordshire, whose family comes from the York area, and the work was directed by Jennifer Hall of Walkington, East Yorkshire, who trained at the Royal School of Needlework.

The cloth is used on all festal occasions such as Christmas, Easter and St. Peter's Day, the Minster's patronal festival. During the tragic fire in the South Transept in 1984, the cloth sustained considerable water damage which resulted in marked shrinkage at one end, but one can only be thankful that it was not totally lost. This was largely owing to its early removal from the altar by the Dean and the Headmaster of the Song School.

The central design on the front of the cloth is an angel holding a tablet on her knee. On the tablet is a ship surrounded by the Greek word *OIKOUMENE*. The ship has been used as a symbol since early Christian times to represent the Church in which the faithful are carried over the stormy seas of life. The World Council of Churches has taken this ship as its emblem, with a cross at the mast and the Greek word *OIKOUMENE*, meaning the Universality of the

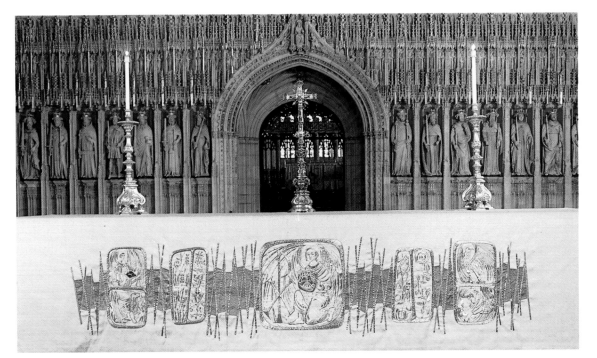

FIGURE 54A   *Festal frontal, Nave altar, Yorkshire Federation of Women's Institutes (front) 1970.*

Church. This emblem makes a focal point of the whole design and is especially fitting for a frontal for the large Nave altar when combined services are held on Festal occasions and all denominations are gathered together.

The central motif also incorporates the *CHI RHO* (☧) which is the earliest monogram of Christ, being the first two letters of the word 'Christ' in Greek.

To the left and right, the Vine, Chalice and Wheat symbolise the Redeemer and the Eucharist whilst the Rose is consecrated to the Virgin and is also applicable to Yorkshire; the Loaves and Fishes come from the parable of the feeding of the five thousand.

The four Evangelists, St. Matthew, St. Mark, St. Luke and St. John, are represented by an Angel or Divine Man, the Winged Lion, the Winged Ox and the Rising Eagle.

On the back of the cloth, the Crowing Cock is one of the symbols associated with St. Peter to whom the Minster is dedicated and the cock also represents repentance. The arms of the Minster formed by the crossed keys under a crown with a Bishop's mitre form the central motif and on the right, the Pelican in her Piety is the symbol of Christ giving Life in His suffering; she feeds her young with blood from her own breast and this represents Our Lord feeding the faithful with His Body and Blood (Figs 55a, b and c).

FIGURE 54B   *Central motif (detail) from the festal frontal.*

On the ends of the cloth are found a Colophon made up of a crowned cross representing the Triumphal Christ with an Orb representing the world and Alpha and Omega, the first and last letters of the Greek alphabet, representing the Beginning and the End.

FIGURE 55A (above left)   *Working drawing for the pelican and chicks.*

FIGURES 55B & C (below left and above)
Completed embroidery of the Pelican's head and chicks.

Zouche Chapel kneelers, 1970

Designed by Edith John, Principal of the Doncaster School of Art and worked by the Minster Broderers in 1970, the designs are based on small quarries of stained glass in the windows of the chapel which show stylised beasts, birds, flowers and tree branches. The best known quarry is that of a wren pecking at a spider in its web (Fig. 56a). Stitches on the kneelers include tent, multiple rice, plaited cross, upright cross, raised oblong cross and Berlin stars (Fig. 56b).

FIGURE 56A (centre right)   *Wren and spider, Zouche Chapel, c.1507.*

FIGURE 56B (right)   *Canvaswork kneeler based on the wren and spider, 1970.*

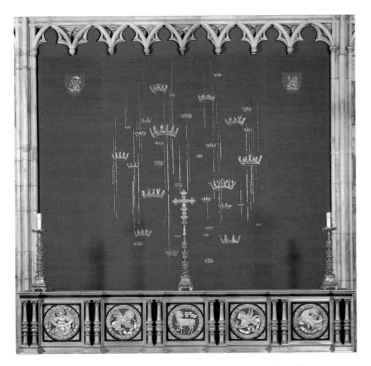

FIGURE 57 *Dossal in All Saints' Chapel, 1974.*

All Saints' Chapel dossal, 1974

All Saints' Chapel is the regimental chapel of The Duke of Wellington's Regiment and was substantially refurnished in 1974. The dossal behind the altar of red Thailand silk was presented in memory of Major General Ozanne, late Colonel of the regiment and his crest of a mailed fist rising from a crown is in the top righthand corner.

The design of crowns, each one different, represents 'all the Saints ascending into heaven'. Designed by Joan Freeman and worked by the Minster Broderers the dossal is worked in laid gold threads, gold kid, cords, beads and some padding (Fig. 57). The regimental cap badge is shown on a shield in the top lefthand corner.

This is the only regiment in the British army with the prefix of a commoner as opposed to that of a member of the Royal family. It was at the express command of Queen Victoria that 33rd/76th Regiment of Foot was renamed The Duke of Wellington's Regiment and it was the Duke's crest which was adapted as the new regimental badge.

Cope, stole and mitre for His Grace, the Lord Archbishop of Canterbury, 1975

These vestments were given to Archbishop Coggan by the Dean and Chapter of York when he was translated from York to Canterbury and were worn by him at his enthronement in Canterbury Cathedral in 1975 (Fig. 58).

The vestments are made of old-gold damask, and at the Archbishop's request, the orphreys of garnet-coloured velvet are embellished with ten coats-of-arms of the school, colleges and dioceses associated with Lord Coggan's life. On the left, from the top, appear the arms of the See of Canterbury, the London School of Divinity, Wycliffe College, Toronto, the See of London and St. John's College, Cambridge. On the right are the arms of the Sees of York and Bradford, Manchester University, Wycliffe Hall, Oxford, and the Merchant Taylor's School, London.

Designed by Joan Freeman with the armorials drawn by Olive Gee, the vestments were worked by the Minster Broderers. The shields are carried out in appliqué, cords, laid gold threads and crochet (for the woolsack on the arms of the See of Bradford).

The vestments are the personal property of the Most Revd the Lord Coggan and are not in the Minster.

FIGURE 58 (above) *Cope and stole for His Grace, the Lord Archbishop of Canterbury, Dr Donald Coggan, 1975.*

FIGURE 59A (below) *Wrought iron screen (detail), All Saints' Chapel.*

All Saints' Chapel kneelers, 1976

Designed by Jennifer Hall and worked by wives and friends of The Duke of Wellington's Regiment, the kneelers were dedicated in 1976.

The design is adapted from the wrought iron screen surrounding the chapel which was itself inspired by a screen in the chapel of the Palazzo Publica in Sienna (Fig. 59a).

The colours of the wools used in the embroidery recall the navy blue uniform of the regiment with its scarlet piping and facings (Fig. 59b).

St. John's Chapel kneelers, 1977

Designed by Joan Freeman and worked by wives and friends of The King's Own Yorkshire Light Infantry Regiment, these kneelers were dedicated in 1977. The regiment was serving overseas at the time the kneelers were being worked, so a simple Florentine pattern was chosen which could be followed from postal instructions (Fig. 60).

The two long kneelers in front of the altar rails repeat the Florentine stitch background, but the central motifs are the regimental monogram, *KOYLI* and the regimental cap badge. Battle honours are worked on the fronts and sides (Fig. 61).

The choice of greens is associated with the regimental green of all Light Infantry regiments and is again echoed in the green of the dossal, *c.*1735–40 (Fig. 21).

FIGURE 59B *Canvaswork kneeler, the design based on the screen for The Duke of Wellington's Regiment, 1976.*

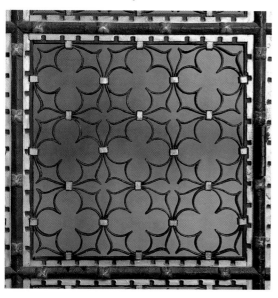

FIGURE 60 (below) *Canvaswork kneeler for the King's Own Yorkshire Light Infantry, St. John's Chapel, 1977.*

FIGURE 61 (above) *Pair of altar rail kneelers for the King's Own Yorkshire Light Infantry.*

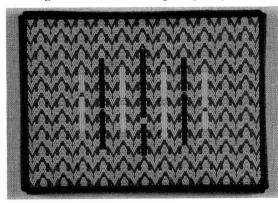

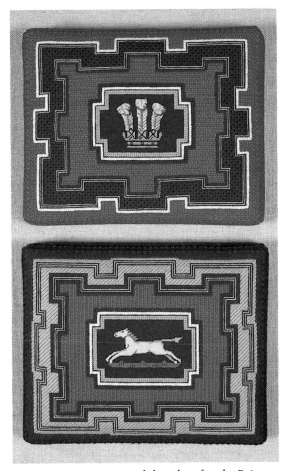

St. George's Chapel kneelers, 1980

These kneelers, which bear two alternative motifs – the Prince of Wales's Feathers and the White Horse of Hanover – were designed by Joan Free-man for the Prince of Wales's Own Regiment of Yorkshire. The present regiment is an amalga-mation of the former East Yorkshire and West Yorkshire Regiments. The choice of colours is based on those of the regimental uniforms but they are used in different ways with the two designs. Worked by wives, friends of the regiment and retired army officers, the kneelers were dedicated in 1980.

FIGURE 62 *Canvaswork kneelers for the Prince of Wales's Own Regiment of Yorkshire, St. George's Chapel, 1980.*

In 1984 the chapel, which is in the South Transept of the Minster, was in the heart of the fire
which destroyed the roof of the transept. None of
the furnishings of the chapel could be rescued
during the fire and consequently everything was
covered with a layer of black carbon dust from
the fallen roof timbers as well as being wet
through from water from the firemen's hoses. In
some cases burning embers and molten lead had
landed on the kneelers, but because they were
already so wet and had been upholstered with
layers of wool carpet felt and not polyurethene
foam, only the whiskers of the wool were singed,
together with one or two superficial burns, and
not one single kneeler was lost. After taking the
kneelers to pieces the canvasses were washed and
re-stretched and then re-upholstered so that little
sign remains of their ordeal (Fig. 62).

FIGURE 63 (below) *Pair of canvaswork kneelers
in St. Stephen's Chapel, 1981.*

FIGURE 64 (right) *Arctic Poppy (detail) from a
kneeler in St. Stephen's Chapel.*

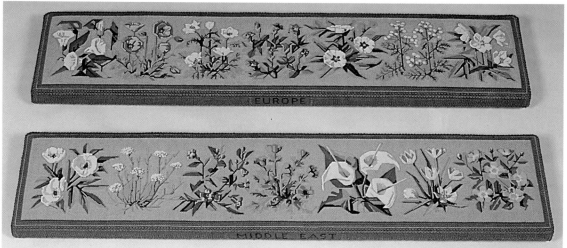

St. Stephen's Chapel kneelers, 1981

St. Stephen's Chapel is used for intercession for
the work of the church overseas and also for heal-
ing services. This was borne in mind when the
kneelers were planned and the theme of flowers
of the world was interpreted by Joan Freeman.
Five pews 2.03m in length fill the centre of the
chapel and these were worked with flowers from
North America and Canada, Australia and New
Zealand, Central and South America, India and
the Far East and Africa. Smaller kneelers continue
the theme for Europe, the Middle East (Fig. 63),
Russia, the Arctic Regions (Fig. 64), England and
Wales, and Scotland and Ireland.

Seventy different flowers are represented, each
slightly stylised but in their natural colours and
worked in tent stitch. The green brick-stitch background and the darker green edges link up with
the colour of the altar frontal (Fig. 29). Worked
by the Minster Broderers and dedicated in 1981.

FIGURE 65   *Festal frontal, High Altar, 1982.*

FIGURE 66   *Dupion stole, goldwork, 1983.*

St. Cuthbert's Chapel altar frontal, 1982

The central regimental badge of The Yorkshire Volunteers was worked by D. E. Moxon-Leeming, Ipswich, and the cloth in scarlet flannel was made up by Jennifer Boyd-Carpenter in 1982.

Festal frontal for the High Altar, 1982

In pink viscose rayon with three foliated crosses dominating the design, the frontal was designed and made by Jennifer Boyd-Carpenter in 1982. The embroidery is of gold threads, gold braids and jewels (Fig. 65).

Gold dupion stole, 1983

The ends of the stole and the nape of the neck are worked in gold thread techniques including *or nué*. Designed and worked by Caroline Grist, Sarah Jones and Rosalie Starling, 1983 (Fig. 66).

St. Nicholas's Chapel kneelers, 1983

Based on the carol, 'The Twelve Days of Christmas', these kneelers were designed by Joan Freeman, worked by the Minster Broderers and dedicated in 1983. Stitches include tent, rice, long arm cross stitch and padded satin stitch (Fig. 67).

Armorial kneelers in the Eastern Crypt, 1983

The Eastern crypt is furnished with three small altars dedicated to St. Hilda, St. Edwin and St. Paulinus. A pair of kneelers in front of each altar bear the attributed arms of the three saints (Fig. 68).

St. Hilda was reputed to be able to turn snakes into stones, hence the design of three coiled snakes. In reality the 'stone snakes' were the ammonites which are found to this day in the cliffs around Whitby where Hilda founded her abbey in AD 657. Ammonites are fossilised sea creatures which have the appearance of coiled snakes.

FIGURE 67 (above)   *Four canvaswork kneelers from St. Nicholas's Chapel, 1983.*

FIGURE 68 (below)   *Three armorial canvaswork kneelers, the Eastern crypt, 1983.*

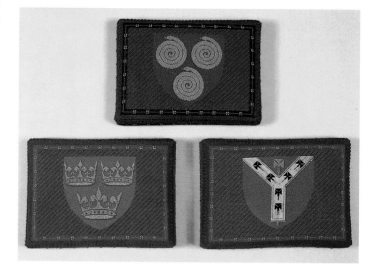

Edwin was King of Northumbria and accepted the Christian faith in AD 627. He was baptised together with all his family at Easter by Bishop Paulinus. A stone church was erected round the wooden church which was the site of the King's baptism, close to the present site of the Minster. The three gold crowns were the King's badge.

After the baptism, which was of considerable significance in the predominantly pagan and Romano-British North-country, the Pope, following the instructions of Gregory the Great that York was to be the seat of the northern metropolitan, alternating in seniority with London, sent to Paulinus the pallium in token of his appointment as archbishop. The pallium did not arrive until after King Edwin was slain in battle c.633 and Bishop Paulinus had fled to the South. The pallium, when it did arrive, was laid up in the church at Rochester in Kent and the establishment of the archbishopric of York was delayed for another hundred years, but London never became an archbishopric at all.

The pallium is a Y-shaped stole which rests across the shoulders with a single falling-band in the centre of the front and back. By tradition it is woven from the wool of sheep which have grazed on the Palatine hills round Rome. The pallium is still in use in the Catholic church and the Pope may be seen wearing it on many occasions.

The pallium worked on the kneelers for St. Paulinus's altar is embroidered in natural hand-spun sheep's wool with a grey fleck, in the spirit of the old tradition. Completed 1984.

FIGURE 69A (below) *The Richardson copes, joining the orphrey sections.*

FIGURE 69B (right) *Completing the embroidery on the Richardson copes.*

The Richardson Memorial copes, 1985

Made by the Minster Broderers as their own commemoration for Alan Richardson, KBE, Dean of York 1964–75, this set of copes was dedicated on St. Peter's Day, 1985.

The copes are of deep coral damask with orphreys of gold Thailand silk. The orphreys each bear a different text which is emphasised by the designs at the foot. Worked in laid gold threads and filosel silks highlighted with citrines and amethysts, each orphrey was worked in three sections which were then seamed together (Fig. 69a), the embroidery being continued over the finished seams (Fig. 69b).

The gilded boss on the morse is taken from the central boss in the central tower of the Minster and shows St. Peter and St. Paul holding a model of the Minster.

The stoles bear the cross of St. Cuthbert worked round a central garnet which recalls Dr Richardson's years in Durham. The emblems of the four Evangelists and the head of St. Paul adorn the ends of the stoles. Designed by Joan Freeman.

FIGURE 70 *One of a set of five copes made in memory of Dr Alan Richardson, Dean of York 1964–75. Dedicated 1985.*

Cope, stole and mitre for His Grace, the Lord Archbishop of York, 1985

At the request of Archbishop Habgood, the cope is of old-gold damask with red orphreys and lining. The design on the orphreys and morse incorporate the white and red roses of the Northern Province whilst the hood bears the arms of the See of York surrounded by a shield-shaped panel of white and red roses.

The stole and mitre each bear the reversed cross of St. Peter. Peter died in Rome where he was scourged and crucified and at his own request he was crucified head down as he did not consider he was worthy to die in the same way as Christ.

The panels of roses are worked in *or nué*, the arms of the See of York in laid silver and gold threads.

The ends of the stole and the lappets of the mitre are edged with a very narrow band of tablet-woven red and gold braid. This is a facsimile of the braid found in the tomb of Archbishop Walter de Gray who died in 1255. The narrow braid had

FIGURE 71 *Cope and stole for His Grace, the Lord Archbishop of York, Dr John Habgood, 1985.*

been attached to the end of one of the wider tablet-woven braids described on p. 20 (Fig. 7a).

Designed by Joan Freeman and worked by the Minster Broderers, these vestments were completed in 1985 and are the personal property of His Grace the Lord Archbishop of York, Dr John Habgood (Figs 71 and 72).

Zouche Chapel, Lenten array, 1986

The altar frontal together with chasuble, stole, burse and veil were designed by Joan Freeman and worked by the Minster Broderers. The instruments of the Passion are carried out in laid cords made from hand-spun, natural sheep's wool from nine different breeds and cross-breeds to obtain graduations in colour from charcoal grey, through chocolate brown to pale greys and fawns. Some filosel silks have been used especially for the coral-coloured crosses. Dedicated in 1986 (Fig. 73).

FIGURE 72 (above)   *Cope (hood) and mitre for Dr John Habgood.*

FIGURE 73 (below)   *Lenten frontal and vestments, Zouche Chapel, 1986.*

Song School banner, 1987

Designed and worked by Jennifer Solomon, the main inspiration for the design was the present York Minster School's link with a Song School at York going back to the Anglo-Saxon period. Thus the central cross is inspired by an Anglian brooch found in York; the lettering is a very free interpretation of that practised by Alcuin, York's most famous Anglo-Saxon scholar; and there is a limited amount of interlaced design, such as one finds in Anglo-Saxon manuscripts.

The five concentric circles represent a musical stave to suggest the important part played by music at the school, though the music in the design is taken from a fifteenth-century antiphoner belonging to York which employed a four-line stave. The notes selected are set to the words *Gloria in excelcis Deo*, an appropriate reference for a religious foundation. Other symbols refer to the present-day life of the school.

The design is worked on red Thai silk which echoes the school colour, and the colours used in the cross are meant to suggest the bronze, overlaid with the patina of years, and the red and yellow enamel of the original brooch (Fig. 74). Presented by Mr and Mrs C. J. Solomon, 1987.

FIGURE 74   *Banner made for the York Song School, 1987 (detail).*

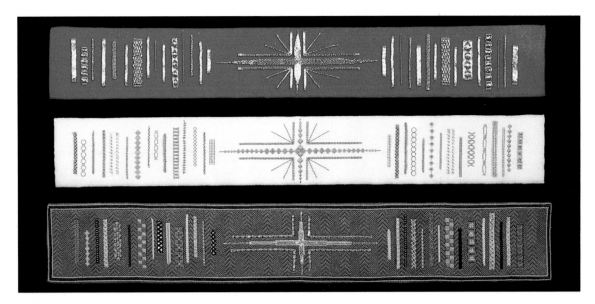

FIGURE 75 (above)   *Three apparel 1987.*

FIGURE 76 (left)   *Frontal for St. Michael's altar (detail) 1987.*

Apparel, 1987

Sets of apparel to be worn by the crucifer, taperers and acolyte have been worked in red Thai silk with laid gold threads, natural linen embroidered in pulled and counted threads and blue, worked on fine canvas (22 threads to the inch), using filosel silks and metallic threads. The design for the three sets is the same, but the differing techniques produce interesting results. Completed in 1987 (Fig. 75).

St. Michael's altar frontal, 1987

The altar stands to the East of the tomb of Archbishop Walter de Gray in the South transept and above it is a stained glass window of St. Michael slaying the dragon. A canvaswork altar frontal, designed by Joan Freeman, is being worked *en suite* with the kneelers flanking the tomb (see p. 19 and Fig. 6b) and the central panel shows the dragon pierced by St. Michael's sword. To be completed in 1987 (Fig. 76).

Glossary

Alb Long white basic garment worn by ministers assisting at the *Eucharist*. It is usually worn with an *amice*.

Amice White neckcloth worn under the *alb*.

Apparel Embroidered band which can be attached to the *amice*.

Bands Two small oblong pieces of white linen with a fastening round the neck, and falling under the chin. Today bands fasten under the chin and not round the neck.

Banner Usually embroidered or woven with sacred symbols and carried in church processions or hung in the church.

Cassock Basic garment worn by clergy, servers and choristers.

Chalice Cup to contain the wine at *Holy Communion*.

Chasuble Sleeveless *vestment* worn over an *alb* during the celebration of *Holy Communion*.

Chimere Sleeveless outer garment worn open in front by bishops and archbishops and black or scarlet in colour: the red *chimere* is also worn by clergy who are not bishops but hold a doctor's degree.

Colophon An orb representing the world with a crowned cross representing the Triumphant Christ.

Commonwealth Rule by Parliament in Britain after the execution of Charles I.

Communion also *Holy Communion*. Enactment of Christ's words and actions at the Last Supper.

Cope Long cloak which is the principal *vestment* worn for ceremonial occasions.

Corporals (*Corporaxes*) Small linen cloths used to cleanse the *Communion* vessels.

Cravat A wide band of white linen folded and tied high round the neck.

Dalmatic Similar in shape to the *alb*, but shorter.

Deacon Assistant to the celebrant at *Holy Communion*.

Dossal/Dorsal Hanging behind an altar.

Eucharist Holy Communion.

Frontlet/Superfrontal Narrow band decorating the top of an altar frontal.

Hassocks *see* **Kneelers**

High Mass Celebration of *Holy Communion* with a celebrant assisted by a *Deacon* and *SubDeacon* with full choral service.

Hood Head covering on the back of a *cope* which may be pulled forward when required. Many copes have vestigial flat hoods only, or no hoods at all. Also the sign of academic degree worn with the *surplice*; of different pattern according to the degree and university.

Kneelers/Hassocks Cushions on which to kneel in church.

Laudian Frontal Named after Archbishop Laud who, in 1604 decreed that the altar must be covered with a 'decent carpet of silk'. Carpet was the normal description of a table covering and the throw-over altar cloth was adapted from it.

Low Mass Celebration of *Holy Communion* by a priest only.

Maniple Loop of material carried over the left wrist. Originally a square of linen used to wipe sacramental vessels and carried in the hand.

Mass Service of *Holy Communion*.

Mitre Traditional headpiece worn by bishops and archbishops.

Morse Fastening at the front of a *cope*, often highly decorated.

Orarium *see* **Stole**

or nué Literally shading in gold. The gold threads are stitched down with contrasting threads and by adjusting the closeness of the stitches, graduations in the colours can be achieved.

Orphrey Decorative vertical bands on *vestments* and frontals.

Oxford Movement A revival of the Catholic tradition in the Anglican church.

Pallium/Pall Y-shaped *stole* conferred by the Pope on Catholic Archbishops before their enthronement. A special mark of rank.

Pall This word has alternative meanings. A stiffened square of white linen placed on the *chalice* during *Holy Communion. Funeral pall* – a large material cover laid over the coffin. It may be suitably decorated.

Pulpit Preacher's desk.

Puritan Dissenter from the Church of England during the 16th and 17th centuries.

Quarry Small piece of glass in a leaded window.

Requiem A *Mass* for the dead.

Riddel Curtain hanging at the side of an altar, often in conjunction with a *dossal*.

Rochet White linen *vestment* similar to an *alb* but worn by bishops and archbishops. The sleeves are full and gathered into a wrist band.

Ruff Stiff pleated band round the neck, some being very elaborate.

Sacerdotal Priestly.

Scarf A black, broad piece of material, usually silk, worn round the neck and hanging down straight in front; part of choir dress for the clergy.

Sisters of Bethany The Society of the Sisters of Bethany. The mother convent is in Bournemouth, Dorset.

Stole Long *scarf* worn over the left shoulder by deacons and over both shoulders by priests. It is the sign of the priest's authority and is one of the *eucharistic vestments*.

Subdeacon The second assistant at *High Mass*. Neither the *deacon* nor the *subdeacon* needs to be a *priest*.

Sudarium Towel or linen napkin originally used by the priest to wipe his face and hands during the service (*sudor* – sweat). It may sometimes be seen wrapped round the metal shaft of a bishop or archbishop's staff on a memorial effigy.

Superfrontal *see* **Frontlet**

Surplice Long, full, flowing vestment of white linen with long, wide sleeves.

Tunicle Similar to the *alb* and *dalmatic* but with slightly different ornamentation. Worn by the *subdeacon*.

Veil Piece of material about 60cm square used to cover the *chalice*.

Vestments Ecclesiastical garments.

Wantage Sisters The Community of St. Mary the Virgin, St. Mary's Convent, Wantage, Oxfordshire.

Further Reading

Richmondshire Churches, H. B. McCall (Elliot Stock, 1910).

The Fabric Rolls of York Minster, J. Raine (ed.) (The Surtees Society, 1859) vol. 35.

Needlework as Art, Lady M. Alford, 1886 (republished by E. P. Publishing Ltd, 1975).

Ecclesiastical Vestments, R. A. S. Macalister (Elliot Stock, 1896).

The Inventory of Church Goods, W. Page (ed.) (The Surtees Society, 1897) vol. 97.

Yorkshire Monasteries Suppression Papers (The Yorkshire Archaeological Society, 1912) vol. 48.

The Reformation in York, 1534–1553, D. M. Palliser, Borthwick Papers, No. 40, (University of York, 1971).

A History of Ecclesiastical Dress, J. Mayo (B. T. Batsford Ltd, 1948).

Ecclesiastical Vestments and Vestmentmakers in York 1300–1600, Sylvia Hogarth, The York Historian , vol. 7, 1986.

Eboracum, (Drake, 1736).

Reformation – Borthwick Paper, York part 3 from Reformation to 1925.

The Journeys of Celia Fiennes, C. Morris (ed.) (Cresset Press, 1947).

A History of York Minster, G. E. Aylmer and Reginald Cant (eds) (Clarendon Press, 1977).

Victoria History of the Counties of England. A History of Yorkshire. The City of York, P. M. Tillott (ed.) (O.U.P., 1961).

The Life of Cosmo Gordon Lang, J. G. Lockhart (Hodder & Stoughton, 1949).

The Shrines of St. William of York, Christopher Wilson (Yorkshire Museum, 1977).

Excavations at York Minster, Derek Phillips (HMSO, 1985) vol. II.

'The tombs of Archbishops Walter de Gray and Geoffrey Ludham', Donald King, *Archaeologia* (Society of Antiquaries, 1971) Vol. 103, Appendix 6.

Norwegian Tapestries (Aase Bay Sjøvold, 1976).

Lives of Nottinghamshire Worthies and of celebrated and remarkable men of the County from the Norman Conquest to A.D. 1882, H. Sotheran (Cornelius Brown, 1882).